HOMETOWN TALES
YORKSHIRE

HOMETOWN TALES is a series of books pairing exciting new voices with some of the most talented and important authors at work today. Each of the writers has contributed an original tale on the theme of hometown, exploring places and communities in the UK where they have lived or think of as home.

Some of the tales are fiction and some are narrative non-fiction – they are all powerful, fascinating and moving, and aim to celebrate regional diversity and explore the meaning of home.

HOMETOWN TALES
YORKSHIRE

CATHY RENTZENBRINK
VICTORIA HENNISON

WEIDENFELD & NICOLSON

First published in Great Britain in 2018 by Weidenfeld & Nicolson
an imprint of The Orion Publishing Group Ltd
Carmelite House, 50 Victoria Embankment
London EC4Y 0DZ

An Hachette UK Company

1 3 5 7 9 10 8 6 4 2

ISBN (Hardback) 978 1 4746 0612 7
ISBN (eBook) 978 1 4746 0613 4

Typeset at The Spartan Press Ltd,
Lymington, Hants

Printed and bound in Great Britain by Clays Ltd, St Ives plc

www.orionbooks.co.uk

CONTENTS

The Yorkshire Years

Cathy Rentzenbrink

CATHY RENTZENBRINK was born in Cornwall and grew up in Yorkshire. She works as a writer and journalist and is the author of *A Manual for Heartache* and the *Sunday Times* bestselling memoir *The Last Act of Love*, which was shortlisted for the Wellcome Book Prize.

'We can never go back again, that much is certain. The past is still too close to us.'

Rebecca by Daphne du Maurier

SETTING OFF

LAST NIGHT I dreamt I went to the Bell and Crown again. I got off the bus at the stop on Selby Road, walked up through the car park and past the garage where my brother Matty kept his old motorbikes. I opened the back door. The pub was empty but the air smelled of cigarettes and beer and was heavy with the promise of friendship and jokes. I headed behind the bar and then down the wide cellar steps. I was looking for Matty. He'd be bottling up. I called for him but there was no answer. Something damp and soft hit me in the face. I'd walked into a brace of pheasants hanging from a hook in the ceiling. There was blood on the shiny feathered breast and a beady dead eye looked out at me through the gloom.

When I woke up I was confused. Light was shining through the curtains and the room was quiet. My husband, Erwyn, was still asleep next to me, our son,

Matt, yet to wake up and come in with his usual barrage of questions.

This is my life now, I thought. I live in London. Home is a flat in a mansion block built in 1935 that narrowly escaped being bombed during the Second World War. If I pull the curtains in our bedroom, I can see the other blocks, some trees and the pink camellia bush that nudges against our window. A couple of hundred metres further away is the motorway flyover that becomes the M4 heading down to the West Country. We are surrounded by train tracks, and if I look between the two blocks opposite for long enough I can catch a glimpse of the district line train chugging between Richmond and Upminster. Some people find our flats too noisy, but I like being surrounded by people and find the sound of traffic comforting. It helps me know the world is still turning, that people are managing to move around, do their jobs and look after their families.

A few minutes away is a footbridge over the railway lines and then you find the Thames. There aren't many pubs called the Bell and Crown but there is another one here, which seemed like a good omen when we were moving into the area. This Bell and Crown sits on the river and, in summer, is packed with tourists. Just behind it is Rose Cottage, where the novelist Nancy Mitford lived on the cusp of the Second World War, in the early days of her marriage to Peter Rodd. Every time I walk by it I wonder if she used to step out, cross the road and watch the river ebb and flow. Perhaps, when the tide was out, she'd walk down one of the sets of wooden steps to indulge in a spot of impromptu mudlarking, as Matt and I do, using a stick to poke about for treasures in the mud. We find lots of blue and white china and are endlessly fascinated by the fact that we are standing on the bottom of the river bed, that later in the day, when the tide changes, there will be water where our heads are now. I like to look at the riverside houses from this perspective and imagine who lives there and who lived there in the past. Kew Bridge is off to the right. I've seen old photos of when it was crossed by horse and cart. Now the queueing cars inch by alongside the pedestrians on their way to Kew Gardens. This proximity of ducks, geese, literature, history and traffic is what London is all about: beauty and grime sit side by side.

I live in London with my husband and son. I am a writer who walks by the Thames when I am stuck with my words. Yorkshire feels like a long time ago.

And yet, as the dream world faded, and my real world took shape, I realised that it was today that I was going back to Yorkshire, to my former home, the other Bell and Crown, that the car was packed and we were due to leave Matt in the care of my parents before driving north. I was nervous, scared of being ambushed by sadness, not sure I'd be able to handle it. As I lay there, I wondered what it would be like to walk down this particular memory lane.

I thought back to the August night in 1990 when everything changed. I was seventeen and just drifting into sleep in my bedroom above the Bell and Crown when I was dragged back to wakefulness by a commotion in the car park. I'd looked out of my window and a stranger had told me that my brother was in trouble, that I had to come. I'd run downstairs and jumped into his car. Matty had been knocked over, the stranger told me. An ambulance had been called.

I'm forty-four now. It is twenty-seven years since I knelt in the road next to Matty's body, but the memory is as sharp as if it happened yesterday. I can feel the breeze of the night air on my arms as I hold on to Matty's wrist, with my fingers on his pulse. I can picture the men who had formed a protective barrier to warn cars that there was someone lying in the road. I can remember the skill and kindness of the ambulance men who got Matty onto a stretcher and then told me to hop in next to him. They called me 'lass,' which is a term of endearment in Yorkshire. 'Hop in, lass,' they said, and, later, their goodbye, 'Good luck, lass.'

I don't want to start telling the story again. For years it was stuck in my head and heart and then I wrote a book about it all called *The Last Act of Love*. I explained what happened to Matty, that his brain was operated on and that he didn't die but nor did he ever recover. I tried to wrestle onto the page the complex emotions. I described how it felt to sit next to the person I most loved in the world, gradually realising that no amount of chatting or singing or making of mix tapes was going to reverse his terrible brain damage, how it gradually and finally dawned on me that it would have been better if Matty had died on the night he was knocked over and that he would not want to be alive as he was.

It was a hard book to write and I worried it would be too hard to read, but people liked it. I'd included little bits about growing up in Yorkshire and I'd written about pub life, about how I learnt to play dominoes for money and how I won the Snaith and District

Ladies' Darts Championship when I was seventeen. I liked those subjects and especially enjoyed talking about them at literary festivals where people often talk about my big preoccupations of life, death, love and literature, but where chats about fives and threes and late night lock-ins are less easy to come by.

Writing my book also made me feel more fondly towards Yorkshire, by which I mean my experience of living there, but whenever I thought about going back for a visit, I could feel the resistance in me. I was frightened, scared of what I'd remember, scared of how I'd feel. I realised that the very word 'Yorkshire' had become twinned in my mind with all the bad and sad things that had happened there.

But I wanted to overcome it, and that's what this trip was about. I'd briefly been back when my book came out. I'd been interviewed in the pub by the BBC's *Look North*, sitting under a cabinet full of darts trophies, and then filmed walking up and down the street outside. It passed in a blur and I wanted to go there again without anyone watching, a trip that would be just for me. I was going to stay in the Bell and Crown as the guest of the current landlord, Ray. I was going to see old friends and walk around.

I wanted to reclaim Yorkshire and no longer feel frightened of either the word or the place.

Later that morning we said goodbye to Matt and my parents and got in the car. Erwyn asked me for the postcode for the SatNav. I stared at him. I couldn't remember it. I tried to imagine writing it as part of my address. I lived there in that almost unimaginable era before email, laptops and smart phones, so I used to write and receive real letters on all kinds of colourful stationery. I pictured a purple envelope and tried to see the address on it. No good. I imagined a sheet of paper and tried to feel the pen in my hand as I wrote the address at the top. The Bell and Crown, Snaith, Nr Goole, East Yorkshire. The postcode wouldn't come. Then I thought of my friends Frank and Liz who live nearby. They send cards and presents to Matt and we send them thank-you cards back. Their postcode starts DN14. The rest came back to me: DN14 9HE. The DN stands for Doncaster.

Erwyn entered it. 194 miles. 3 hours and 12 minutes. I was going home.

WHERE ARE YOU FROM?

THIS IS A question I get asked all the time as people try to pin down my accent and work out where my surname comes from. I have a three-pronged minimum answer. I was born in Cornwall, I grew up in Yorkshire and I now live in London. If the conversation continues, I'll say that my father is Irish and I have turns of phrase that come from him and then I married a Dutchman – hence the unusual name. My son is half-Dutch, a quarter Irish and a quarter Cornish. I've lived in different parts of the world. I didn't think of myself as having Irish looks until my time in New York and Chicago when I was continually told I must be Irish by enthusiastic and affectionate strangers. I'm a linguistic chameleon and my voice morphs to match the people I'm speaking to. Sometimes I feel happy about this and think it is indicative of my interest in my fellow humans, other times I worry it's part of a craven desire to fit in at all costs.

Is Yorkshire home, then? I don't feel like I'm from Yorkshire, but then I don't feel like I'm from anywhere else. I'm more Yorkshire than I am Cornish or Irish, though I have no blood connection to the place. If my parents hadn't decided to retire down to Cornwall, I'd have carried on visiting them in Yorkshire so I'd feel more connected. I live in London but I don't feel like a Londoner. I'm never sure I'm here to stay. Perhaps it is because living in a flat doesn't seem completely grown-up. For his fourth birthday Matt asked for some string, some blue tack, some Bob the Builder stickers and a house with stairs, with no real understanding that some of those things were easier to come by than others. My friends and relatives who don't live in London do live in houses with stairs and driveways, and gardens with sheds, greenhouses, fishponds and barbecues. That seems like grown-up life to me, and I wonder whether we'll eventually leave London for the lure of more room and a less frantic pace of life.

*

My first memory of Yorkshire is from the day we arrived. I was five, Matty was four, and it was summer. We'd been living in a bungalow and were so excited to have our own set of stairs that we kept running up and down them. There were four bedrooms. Mum and Dad got the biggest, the next was to be a spare room – for years we were allowed to bounce on the spare room bed as a Sunday night treat – and that left the two smallest for me and Matty. Mine was a little larger but his had a wall cupboard I would come to envy. I have a thing about built-in cupboards and like filling them up with books and stationery. I still dream about this one, that I'm in there looking for Matty but can't find him, or that I've filled it up with all my stuff and he's cross with me.

In the front garden there was a rockery. I sat under the trees and watched the way the leaves made shadows on the grass. I looked up at the sky. My parents and brother were in the house. The windows were open and Gerry Rafferty's voice was drifting into the air. I was happy and expectant. I don't remember feeling sad that we'd left Cornwall and that I'd have to go to a new school. I was excited at the prospect of making new friends.

Years later – about thirty-five years later – I will

tell this memory to a therapist. She will find it significant that I am apart from my family and will make me draw a picture of it. I will give it a go but then get frustrated and scribble across it. She'll find that significant, too. I'll say that I can't draw and don't see the point of looking for a non-existent dark side of a pleasant memory. 'I had a happy childhood,' I'll say, 'that's not the problem.'

I decide to find out more about how we ended up in Yorkshire in the first place. What were the steps that led my Cornish mother and my Irish father to bring their little family to this corner of England to grow up under the power stations?

How did I come to grow up in Yorkshire?

BEFORE YORKSHIRE

I CAME INTO existence because of a storm at sea in 1966. My dad was a deck boy on a German merchant ship making her way from Dagenham to Cork. Dad had run away to sea when he was fifteen and after a couple of days of throwing up on his first voyage out he'd learnt to love the life of seeing new places and meeting and working alongside interesting people. He also enjoyed doing work he felt good at. He'd run feral after the death of his mother and had stopped going to school because he was teased for being dirty. He'd got used to the idea of himself as stupid and troublesome but his practical talents came to the fore once at sea and he liked the discipline on offer. After a few months working alongside the mainly German crew he could speak their language fluently and thought he might not be so stupid after all. He also loved earning money. After years of poverty and

17

humiliation – most of his early memories involve the pawn shop queue – he delighted in having his own money in his pocket.

The first time my dad saw Falmouth was when the ship had turned back from Land's End to the nearest safe port after a force ten south-westerly had ripped the cargo from the decks. The storm had been forecast but the captain had hoped to get across to Ireland before it hit. My dad thought it was strange how the captain always set out for Cork whatever the weather, yet wouldn't leave Cork if the forecast was above a force seven. Later he learnt there was a girl in the Laurel Bar who the Captain wanted to be with. Such are the coincidences that make us happen. Were it not for the Captain's affair, my dad would not have seen Falmouth that day, not have fallen for the calm beauty of the place after the danger of the storm, and not have pledged to make time to go back there for a holiday.

He was eighteen when he made the trip back and my mum was fourteen. They met on Custom House Quay. She fell in love with him from the start. It was his voice that hit her first, a lilting mix of southern Irish with a continental twang from his time speaking only German on the ship. He was unlike anyone she had ever met. Most of her friends were dating boys from the grammar school, but he was older, working on a ship, had been to sea, and came from a different country. My grandmother was less impressed, and would have preferred Mum to be interested in a boy with parents and homework and rules, and not be besotted with this tattooed Irish sailor who drank in pubs, could hardly read and write, had long hair and drove a motorbike. My dad was love-struck too and painted Mum's nickname 'Moggs' on the jetty at the docks in huge white letters, visible to everyone when the tide was right.

When Dad went back to sea, he left Mum his deposit book and each time he got into port and was paid he would send a money telegram which she'd pay into his bank. The telegram would say he'd phone that night so she'd walk down to the village phone box, Perran-ar-Worthal 862, and wait for his call.

Even when Dad left the sea for more steady employment, he still had to work away and when I came along, and then my brother a year or so later, they wanted the family to be together. They bought a caravan and we travelled from job to job with Dad, towing our little home behind the Land Rover.

Sometimes we'd be in the middle of a field, sometimes in the heart of a town. Residents were often a bit worried when we arrived but once they knew Dad was employed by the engineering company Costains, and that we would soon be moving on, they relaxed. If we stayed anywhere for any length of time then a social worker would turn up and Mum would have to show that we were being looked after. Which we were. Dad could access the fire hydrants and fill up our tank of water, and a little gas geyser gave us hot running water. There are photos of me and Matty being bathed in the sink at the caravan. We were fat and happy. You can see the love shining out of my parents. My dad is all beard and twinkly eyes; my mum is wand-thin, her long hair often in a plait. There are two photos I especially like of them sitting on the bonnet of the Land Rover. Mum is wearing a pair of purple loons.

They flirted with the idea of moving to Australia and liked the notion of being in a new land, so when an opportunity arose to go to the Shetland Islands with Foundation Engineering they took it. Shetland was booming and the prospects looked good. The caravan was shipped to a site just outside Hillswick and we flew up from London via Aberdeen. I was eighteen months old and delighted that the friendly air hostess gave me a colouring book and some pencils.

We settled in well. There was a huge drinking culture on the Island, not just in the pubs, but everywhere. Many of the local men carried a half bottle in their jacket pocket and a trip to the local shop would often turn into a long session. Visitors would be offered rum, served in glasses almost full, with just a splash of coke on top.

When a nearby croft came up for sale, my parents decided to buy it. They had plans drawn up to renovate the derelict cottage and towed our caravan out to Hamar Voe, pleased to be living for the first time on their own land.

The neighbouring croft was owned by an old widower, who lived there with his daughter and teenage granddaughter. The girls were delighted to have new people to talk to but the old man was not so keen. He was cantankerous with everybody, though, especially his daughter who seemed to do all the work. There was a son who came home from time to time, and although the old man and his son seemed to hate each other, they were united in their dislike of incomers. Things came to a head when a vehicle had got stuck in the mud by the gate to the croft. Dad helped to free it and later overheard the man talking about him as 'that useless foreign wanker'. Mum and Dad realised we were always going to be considered outsiders and that the clean air, beautiful landscape and buoyant economy were no good if we didn't feel welcome. We headed back down to Cornwall.

I have no memories of life on Shetland. I was too little. When my son was born and I'd watch my parents cuddle him, singing to him and bouncing him, I felt like I was seeing my own past. I can imagine us all there in the caravan: tucked up, warm and safe. My dad singing us Irish songs about people who travel far and wide, not always willingly – 'The Black Velvet Band', 'Whiskey in the Jar' and 'The Bold Thady Quill'. My mum cooing nursery rhymes – 'Round and round the garden, like a teddy bear', a couple of Cornish songs, 'Lamorna' and 'Going up Camborne Hill, coming down'.

I'd always known I'd lived on Shetland for a few months as a toddler, but I hadn't known the plan had been to stay there, until I was telling my parents how excited I was to be doing an event in Orkney and the subject came up. When I made that trip, almost forty years after we left Shetland, I sat in Orkney library and learnt from the audience that Orkadians refer to everywhere else as 'South'. We pondered together that had I, in another universe, grown up on Shetland, all of them would have been south of me. In the morning I walked around the harbour breathing in the air and wondering how it would have been. Would it have kept Matty safe, if we'd stayed on Shetland? What sort of a person would I have become if our next door neighbour had been less grumpy? Talking this over with my dad afterwards, he said, 'Yes, life would have been very different if I hadn't seen red with him. I had a bit of a Roy Keane moment. A mist came down.'

After leaving Shetland, we went back to Cornwall, finally settling in Lanner, a little village just two miles from my grandparents' house. I started at primary school, and Dad got a job at Mount Wellington tin mine. The job was hard and dangerous, but Dad loved it, and he especially loved that it was the best paid work in the county. He worked all the hours he could, and on the weekends always signed up for the 'spillage' shifts – eight hours of shoveling the silt from the bottom of the shaft so that there was room for the cage to be lowered to collect the ore during the next week. One Sunday, in the summer of 1978, when the spillage shift had been cancelled, we had a day out to the village of St Mawes, catching the passenger ferry from Falmouth and landing on the pretty granite quay. We ate our pasties on the beach, and while my brother and I went rock-pooling, my parents sunbathed against the sea wall and talked about how life was good and how they were managing to save a lot of money. What should they do with it all?

The next day, Dad arrived at work and was told the mine was closing down. The price of tin had collapsed because it could be mined much more cheaply abroad. Cornish tin was no longer viable.

Dad got a redundancy payment equivalent to six weeks' wages, giving him time to look for a new job. He could go back to his old work – site investigation – but that would mean being on the road again, and now my brother and I had reached school age we wouldn't be able to travel as a family. The government had supplied funding for the mine to be pumped dry for three months while a rescue plan was negotiated, and Dad was re-employed as a pump man. It gave us a temporary fix, but there was no future or money in it and Dad knew he needed to find something else.

A week after the closure of Mount Wellington a possible solution arrived. The Selby coalfield was starting up and shaft sinkers were needed. The tin miners, who were experienced in drilling and blasting, were ideal, and they were called for interview at the Redruth Employment Exchange. Instead of the grueling interview he was expecting, Dad was asked what job he wanted. He was proud that people knew of him, that he had a good reputation. He asked for Shaft Captain and was offered it. Dad and Mum were invited up to Yorkshire to see the area so they left us with our grandparents and stayed two nights at The Black Bull in Escrick, near York. They liked what they saw – rural but not remote – and the job promised well-paid secure employment for years to come. They viewed a few houses and decided on a four-bedroom modern house in Carlton with no buying chain. Our house in Lanner was bought by the first people who came to see it, and within weeks we had moved to Yorkshire.

My mother documented all of our moves in the back page of my baby book so I know that I lived in thirty-five separate places before I was five, including London, Barnstaple, Torquay, South Shields and Westward Ho! The last entry on the list is August 1978: To 22 Almond Tree Avenue, Carlton, Goole.

IN TRANSIT

ERWYN DROVE US out of London, past the grimy houses that line the North Circular, and then up the M1. As we arrived in Yorkshire, I asked him if he'd ever been there before. He's Dutch, but has been living in the UK since 2000, and had a life here before we knew each other. He'd been to York for a couple of short trips for work but that was it.

'I guess it's not dissimilar to Holland in the feel of the land,' I said, as we drove past green fields, sheep and cows. People think of the dales and the moors when they hear Yorkshire, but our bit is flat. 'Though the roads are bendy,' I said nervously as Erwyn took a corner slightly too fast. 'No Dutch straight roads here. Some of these corners are deceptively vicious.'

As we got nearer, we saw the first power station. I grew up in the shadow of the power stations and still find the sight of them comforting: the chimneys with their welcoming plumes, the white puffs that scrawl across the sky. The towers sit in grey-bricked clusters of six or eight. Ferrybridge, Eggborough, Drax. 'Drax – that sounds like a sexually transmitted disease,' someone once said to me when I was far from home and describing where I lived. A dose of the Drax. These three power stations form a triangle of coal burning and electricity churning, but underneath there are patchwork squares of hay-stacked fields knitted together by country lanes.

'We're a long way from London,' I said, nodding at all the tractors on the road. There were bunches of flowers tied into hedges, fences and bridges to mark fatal accident sites. One of these tributes included several blue and yellow scarves and rosettes from Leeds United Football Club.

I saw that the Bay Horse in Cowick had been turned into an Indian restaurant. The pub was on our dog walking route and there used to be a sign in the car park that said, 'Coaches welcome', the optimism of which made us giggle.

We drove on past Cowick Hall, once a stately home, now known as Croda due to the chemical company housed there. Matty used to play football in the surrounding fields. As we drove around the bend into Snaith I saw new houses near the bus stop where I'd wait to be taken to sixth form college in Scunthorpe. I'd chosen to go there rather than the nearer options of Selby or Goole because I wanted to do Theatre Studies. That seems very odd to me now, though perhaps it shouldn't as I enjoy all the aspects of my professional life that include an element of performance.

Nearly there. We passed the Plough Inn, the Black Lion, the butchers. It all looked the same. I directed Erwyn down the narrow street that leads to the car park around the back of the pub and we pulled in. There it was, the Bell and Crown, scene of much of my early life and of that morning's dream. I needed a couple of steadying breaths.

We parked up in front of the bungalow extension we'd built when it became clear that Matty wasn't going to get better and that none of the hospitals wanted to keep him. We'd had to knock down the old garage where Matty used to fix motorbikes and do science experiments to allow for a building with ramps and doors wide enough to allow his hoisted body to pass through safely. A picture of Matty flashed into my mind. Imagine a six foot four man with no ability to move of his own accord curled up in a big sling suspended from a metal hoist so he could be pushed between bed and the shower trolley and the sofa and back to bed. At the time, we were fiercely focused on finding a home to look after him where we could keep him safe, but eventually I saw the crazy side of building a one-man hospital for a person who would rather not be alive anyway.

I got out of the car and realised I was standing a few feet from where Matty died, one Sunday afternoon all those years ago. I wasn't there. Matty had been in a permanent vegetative state for so long with no hope of him getting better, so we had taken the decision to withdraw treatment. It took longer than we'd been told to expect and I found it unbearable. After ten days, my heart breaking, I returned to London and was there when Dad phoned three days later to tell me Matty was gone.

As we walked on through the beer garden, I remembered other long, sunny Sunday afternoons full of drink and jokes. That was the constant juxtaposition of our pub world. We lived a cheek by jowl existence where fun and despair were constant companions. It was a master class in putting on a brave face. I'd be sitting with Matty, looking into his vacant eyes, desolate as I gradually realised he was never coming back, and then I'd have to go and do a shift behind the bar. I'd have only a few steps to get a smile on my face and be ready to pull pints and laugh at jokes and I always managed it.

There's an outside smoking terrace, now, another sign of the times. I never smoked behind the bar, but when it wasn't busy I'd sit the other side on a bar stool, smoking fags with my favourite customers.

I opened the back door and was hit with the familiar morning smell of booze cut with the scent of bleach. A barmaid I didn't recognise gave us a warm welcome and showed us upstairs. We walked through the back kitchen, up the back stairs and past Matty's bedroom. She showed us into the main bedroom which looks over the main street. My parents had this one when we first moved in, and I took it over at some point after they'd gone down into the bungalow. Everything was the same but different. The bed was on the other side of the room. I looked out of the window on to the main street and the pub across the road, the Downe Arms. How many times had I done this in my life? When we first moved in, my friends and I would be glued to the upstairs windows so we could track the movement of the boys we fancied between the two pubs.

I remembered the wall safe. Still there, behind the wardrobe. Open, so that any intruder could see it wasn't worth trying to break into it. I used to have nightmares that I'd closed it by accident and that the men who'd broken in wouldn't believe that I'd forgotten the code and it was empty anyway.

In the bathroom I thought about the morning after the accident when we came back from the hospital, how I washed Matty's blood off my hands in the bath as his dog Polly looked sadly on. I'd told Polly he'd be OK, but he never was and she pined away without him. I wanted to travel back in time and comfort my younger self, but then, would she want to hear anything I had to say? What would I say? I couldn't tell her everything would be OK. You will survive this, I could tell her. That would be honest. You will survive this.

'I don't care about me,' she'd say, 'What about Matty? Is he going to die?'

'He is,' I could say, 'Though not for a long time. You'll come to desire his death you know. You'll come to want it more than anything else.'

'No I won't.'

Our conversation breaks down. My younger self

is bolshy and resilient and does not want my advice. She is not ready.

'I promise you that in your future you are glad to be alive.'

She gives me a look. She doesn't need this yet, either.

I know, I think. Books, quotes. 'Are you reading Maya Angelou yet?'

She shakes her head.

'She's good in adversity. Also, there's this French saying that you will come to love. *La vie s'arrange, mais autrement.* Life works out, but not as you think.'

She nods.

And Viktor Frankl: 'Everything can be taken from a man but one thing: the last of the human freedoms – to choose one's attitude in any given set of circumstances, to choose one's own way.'

'OK.'

I left her there.

I found more traces of myself in a bookcase in the corridor. Adrian Mole and Kathy Acker. A dictionary looked familiar. I opened it. My dictionary. Cathy Mintern, 1 Howard, it said on the flyleaf in the neat handwriting of a hardworking eleven-year-old girl who loves learning and coming top of the class. There were three houses at my secondary school: Howard, Hinsley and Beaumont. All named for various Catholic aristos or dignitaries. I've changed my name twice since then. Cathy Mintern is long gone, only a name in an old dictionary. I wondered what she'd make of me being an actual writer with books of my own on people's shelves.

I looked down the wide staircase that leads from the upstairs directly down into the bar. Before we built the bungalow, we had to carry Matty up and down it. More than once after a massive epileptic fit, he'd be stretchered down it by paramedics into a waiting ambulance, past all the people drinking and playing darts.

Ghosts. I was surrounded by ghosts. I didn't feel any presence of Matty here, but a cacophony of my former selves.

'Come on,' I said to Erwyn, 'Let's go for a walk.'

A WALK THROUGH CARLTON

WE WALKED OUT of the back door again, across the car park and down to the main road. The bus stop looked just the same as it always did. Once an hour you can catch the 401 to Selby. If you get on it going the other way, it will take you to Goole.

We walked past the railway crossing, 'That's the shelter where Matty and I used to go and smoke pot. One night the wind gusted everything away and we had to give up and go home.' I felt like an old person telling this story. There's probably a whole new language that the kids use now and I don't know any of the words. I remembered the excitement and confusion of using them in the first place. I was never good at sums and couldn't ever remember out of an eighth or a sixteenth which was bigger.

There were new reinforcements on the bridge that stands over the river Ouse connecting the two villages.

Carlton people call it Snaith Bridge, and Snaith people call it Carlton Bridge. I told Erywn the story of the young man who decided to commit suicide by throwing himself off the bridge, climbed up to the top but then changed his mind and couldn't get down so had to ring 999 from up there. I remember people weren't very sympathetic, and he was in general viewed as a bit of an attention seeker – not a quality that impresses Yorkshire people – and he owed quite a lot of money. Nobody believed he'd ever meant to do it. He left the area fairly soon afterwards.

We stood on the bridge looking down at the riverbank where my brother Matty tried to teach me how to ride his motorbike and I fell off. Up river is the old bridge, a collection of pillars I remember sketching on an outing from school. A few more steps and we were in Carlton.

The first field over the bridge used to be a strawberry field and I was caught stealing strawberries there once. The farmer was nice to us, telling us to take what we had home to our mums and not do it again.

I wanted to show Erwyn Carlton fishponds but it was all gated off. We used to collect conkers here, prising them out of their prickly skins ready for the school competition. There were all sorts of theories about toughening them up with vinegar or by placing them in the airing cupboard. When I was older, we'd go swimming in the pond, the thought of which gives me the shivers now. A few kids, a few old tyres, a rope swing. All under the shade of the trees, so it was freezing cold even in the summer. It sounds like the set-up for one of those novels where the heroine remembers a ghastly secret like an accident that was no accident. Nothing bad happened though. Later, I used to go pea picking in the fields just behind. Back-breaking work for not much money, as I remember, though I liked eavesdropping on the conversations of the older pickers, girls who would talk about boyfriends and sex and swear a lot. One of them once said, 'I need to go and shake my lettuce,' and it was only when she came back and explained where the toilets where that I understood what she meant.

The swans were still there. I wondered how long swans live and if it might still be the same pair.

We came to Carlton Towers, a stately home owned by the Duke of Norfolk, where sometimes, for a treat, we were walked up from school to watch the hunt set off. I remember men in red coats on horses surrounded by dogs, all seen from the perspective of a small child not very far from the ground, though my memory is muddled and overlaid with what I now know from reading novels like *The Pursuit of Love* by Nancy Mitford and *Riders* by Jilly Cooper. I think I remember servants offering glasses of sherry on silver trays but it seems a bit unlikely. Can I really remember the men swigging from hipflasks, or do I think I can because I've read about Rupert and Billy?

Our friend, Didge, was the son of the caretaker so we hung around up there quite a lot and I was allowed in the library where I fell in love with the walls full of books. The shelves went up so high that there were special ladders and stools to get at them. There was also a priest's hole. I have always loved both books and history and spending time at The Towers was a huge delight. Matty and Didge weren't interested in any of this. They liked scrubbing around in the woods and eventually went halves on an old Fiat and taught themselves to drive off road. They also entertained themselves by hunting down Didge's father's secret stash of fags – he was supposed to have stopped smoking – destroying them, and then trying to be around so they could witness his frustration when he found out they were gone. The boys were gleeful at having discovered something mean and naughty that they couldn't be punished for, because Didge's dad wasn't supposed to be smoking at all so couldn't even complain about their behaviour to Didge's mum. Hours of fun.

Once a year, the whole village turned out for Carlton Feast and followed the floats of fancy dressed groups – I'd have been with the Brownie float – up the drive for country dancing displays, tombolas and the opportunity to win a goldfish by bouncing a ping pong ball into a glass jar. We had several of these as pets but they never lasted very long. The first one – Goldie – was eaten by our cat, Brandy. Not long afterwards Brandy was run over by next door's car. My dad buried her in the garden and told us she'd gone to live with someone else. A few days later, we were out playing, noted the disturbed earth and dug her up. 'Dad, Dad, the people who took Brandy have killed her and buried her in our garden.'

I've got photos of Matty winning races at Carlton Feast and holding up a big silver trophy. As we got older, Feast day was more about trying to win a bottle of Pomagne from the tombola. We'd sit and share it on the grass and there'd always be some kid who would either actually be drunk or pretend to be. On the same weekend, the fair came to Lockwood's field. The air was sugared by candyfloss and we were bedazzled by the lights and the music, and the way the fair lads could stand up and walk around on the Waltzers.

Carlton Towers is where I married my first husband, John, not far off twenty years ago. It feels like a different country, a different life. The ceremony was in Snaith Church and then we'd hired a double decker bus to get to the Towers. Everyone from my side got very drunk and several people fell over on the polished wooden floors.

Further into the village, we passed the Methodist's Chapel, where we used to go for Christingle, which meant having a satsuma with a candle stuck into it for I'm not sure what reason, but I liked watching the little flames.

We walked by the Oddfellows, the first pub my dad went in when we moved here. He had a set of darts in his pocket, which was the way he'd got used to making friends in England. The first person he met was Frank who, with his wife Liz, is still our dear friend almost forty years later.

The sweetshop where I worked on Sunday afternoons had turned into a hairdressers called Dyenamix. I loved that job. Men came in for cigarettes and mince and onion pies which we heated up in a microwave. Women came in to buy homemade butterfly buns, blocks of cheddar, and for Tampax which always had to be wrapped in a brown paper bag. Everyone came in for sweets. There were large glass jars of them and we had to weigh them out by the quarter. I wish I could remember how much they cost. Cola cubes, pineapples cubes, pear drops, rhubarb and custards: all the boiled sweets were the same price. More expensive were the chocolate limes and peppermint creams. All individually wrapped in shiny paper. Kids never bought them, they were too dear but also too boring, the sort of sweets that old people ate. We also did mixes. Five pence or ten pence mixes. My favourites were the foamy pink shrimps. I also liked sherbet fountains and dib-dabs. There was a bright pink chewy bar called a 'Wham' that would stick your teeth together.

We walked down Pinfold Lane and into Almond Tree Avenue. 'There it is, Number 22.'

A car alarm was going off a few doors down and I worried we looked a bit suspicious. There was probably not much need for strangers to ever come down this street and we looked like we were not from round here. I told Erwyn about how there was this nightclub in Goole where if you got asked the question, 'You're not from round here, are you?', the next stage was a punch in the face. He looked a bit alarmed and I reassured him that Almond Tree Avenue had always been a calm and peaceful place.

I took a quick photo of the house. I could still see where the rockery was. We used to jump out of the spare room window onto the garage roof, which, looking with my new motherly eyes, seems a horribly dangerous endeavor. I remember that the first time we did this, I tricked Matty into going first by telling him that I'd done it before, which I hadn't.

I wished Matt was here so I could show him where I lived when I was his age. As he grows up, he reminds me of my childhood. The way he doesn't want to put his shoes fully on – it's too much like hard work – conjures an image of Matty doing the same thing. I can picture my mum in the hallway, shoe in hand, annoyed because the back is all worn down. Recently, when Matt came home having not eaten much of his packed lunch, I remembered hiding my own uneaten sandwiches in the garage and then having to answer for it when they were found. I said that I hadn't felt well and I'd given away my apple and my United but no one wanted my sandwiches. This wasn't true; I just hadn't wanted the sandwiches.

I told Erwyn this and he told me how he used to throw his uneaten *broodjes* out of his bedroom window, not realizing that they were amassing in the gutter beneath until everything got blocked up and a man had to be called to sort it all out. Kids have such a misplaced confidence in their ability to deceive.

We once planted radishes and carrots in the back garden and none of mine grew because I kept digging them up everyday for a look. Matty's did. He was always less impulsive than me, more patient, better at saving sweets and money. 'Money burns a hole on your pocket,' my dad would say, as I spent up in the toyshop in Selby, while Matty would save for several weeks to buy one big thing, or even put his money in the building society, a level of planning and foresight that I couldn't begin to understand.

Our dog, Polly, was an escape artist. She could open doors, so if someone forgot to turn the key in the lock of the front door she'd be off, and she loved nothing better than to dig tunnels under the back garden fence and go rummaging in the neighbours' bins or scouring the fields for a dead bird to roll in. Matty was best at getting her back. He taught her lots of tricks. We both had jobs that we did in exchange for our pocket money and one of his was to walk Polly before school. Last year, our friend Ian told me that when he'd come round to call for Matty in the mornings, he'd say, 'Just take Polly out for me while I get ready,' and Ian would do so, wondering how he always got lumbered with the jobs that Matty got paid for.

One of Matty's other jobs was filling the coalscuttle. We got free coal because Dad was a shaft-sinker and it was delivered and tipped into the bunker in our garage which was made out of breeze blocks. That was where we kept our pet grass snake, Grassy. He lived in a big glass jar that had to be in sight, on the top of the bunker, so my mother could always check that we hadn't moved him into the house. Eventually we decided it was a bit cruel to keep Grassy so we liberated him on our next trip up to the dales. We collected snails in ice cream cartons and they too were confined to the garage. I'm ashamed to admit we'd forget about them and they'd melt down into a liquidy sludge with bits of shell poking out. I'm not a squeamish eater, but I've never been able to handle escargots. I think the memories of the contents of our neglected Tupperware are too strong in my mind.

I took another look at it, the house with stairs that we grew up in. The phone was on the stairs and Matty and I used to hide on the top landing when Dad was on the phone to work as we loved hearing him swear. He never swore or shouted at us, though the stairs were also the scene of the only domestic dispute I ever remember witnessing – when Dad tripped over Mum's handbag on his way out to work and said, 'What a stupid place to leave a handbag.' That night he came home with Black Magic for Mum and Quality Street for us all to apologise.

Some of our friends who had less happy home lives loved being in our house because there was never any arguing and Mum and Dad were happy to see them and interested in what they had to say about their day at school. It was only when a friend told me how different this was from how things were when she went home that I began to fully appreciate it. As we got older there was often a house full with lots of our friends sleeping over and my mum making bacon sandwiches for everyone in the morning. We wouldn't have called it a sleepover then, of course, nor did we go trick or treating and the Fifth Form disco was yet to be rebranded as Prom Night.

By the time we were in secondary school, my dad

worked shifts at Maltby pit, so when he was on after-noons and had to work from two till ten, we'd come home for lunch and he'd cook us hot dogs with lots of ketchup and fried onions and then there would always be a Fry's chocolate cream or a pack of fruit pastels for pudding. On night shifts, after he'd woken up, he'd walk up to school and watch us play in football, netball and hockey matches. Lots of dads went to watch their sons play football but he was the only dad who came to watch his daughter play hockey.

I also played a lot of darts with Dad when he was on nights. We had a board in our dining room and we'd play endless games of around the clock or 501. There'd be an age appropriate handicap system to make it more fun. With around the clock, he'd have to hit trebles, while I only had to get doubles. In 501, he'd give me a hundred start and the off.

Erwyn and I walked on to the end of the street, me pointing out houses where friends had lived. I'd been thinking about childhood friendships a lot as I helped Matt navigate the ups and downs of the playground. Some of his relationships are nerdy and nourishing, others are more intense. The other day, I explained to him the concept of a 'frenemy' and told him that I'd had friends who always seemed to make me cry, even though I loved them.

My friend Susan, who lived opposite to us, never made me cry and was sweet and dreamy. I loved being with her because she had loads of Pippas, Barbies and Sindys. I had none because my mother didn't herself approve of dolls and I'd never shown any interest in any toys other than books until I hit a stage where I longed to fit in. I loved playing with Susan and her Girl's World, doing hairstyles and dressing them all up.

Later, I had a good portfolio of babysitting jobs in the avenue and beyond, though I was never skilled at looking after children. I didn't enjoy playing with them and found the one job that was more like child-minding – I had to make tea for a five-year-old boy, bath him and put him to bed – to be deeply tedious. I never confessed to this as it was just taken for granted that if you were a girl you would enjoy hanging out with babies and children. Some of my friends used to go and spend time with the kids they babysat just for pleasure, which I could never understand. Once, on fair weekend, when some of my friends were taking the kids they looked after to the fair, I decided I should do the same. I was so bored and couldn't wait to deliver this little boy back to his parents. What I liked about babysitting was talking to the grown-ups, being in charge of the house and, if there were any, having access to the bookshelves. I'd discovered Norah Lofts in one of my houses.

Pointing out the difference in shades of tarmac, I showed Erwyn where our avenue had ended. On one side it was a field of nettles, and I once flew off my bike into them because I forgot how to brake. My friend's older sister had a party trick of taking her hands off the handle bars and clapping them three times above her head while whooping. I thought she was wonderful. One day she fell off mid whoop and went running off in tears to her house, leaving her bike in the middle of the road. I still think of her every time someone says that rather typically York-shire expression, 'Pride goes before a fall.'

The bottom of the avenue was all built up now, the fields behind covered in houses. There used to be a barbed wire fence we'd climb over and then we were off to the dyke, the rope swing and the haystacks behind. There was an old horse box we used to play dares in: 'I dare X to kiss Y etc.' and a machine that had something to do with sugar beet that we'd clam-ber all over. There were bridges to sit under, one of which sometimes had torn pages from porn mags left there. The boys would hold them up, trying to work it all out. The girls would feign lack of interest or disgust. No one wanted to be called a slag, which was the fate of all girls who liked sex. I didn't know what 'slag' meant, so asked an older girl who lived up the street. 'It's like a prostitute but they don't get paid for it,' she told me.

We played outside all day, going home for our lunch and our tea, which we'd bolt down so we could get back out to our mates. There were no children on the street today but it was a school day. I wondered how it would look on the weekends and hoped there would still be groups of kids out sitting on curbstones. I fret about how to provide unsupervised yet safe-ish play for Matt. He's never out of the sight of an adult, he and his little friends never have the space to fall out with each other and make up without a grown-up intervening to guide them. I'm not sure how much this is a general sign of the times or specific to London and city life.

'Come on,' I said to Erwyn. 'I'll take you to my school by the route I used to walk.'

We walked back up the avenue to the alleyway. It

felt tiny. The signpost said 'Convent Walk' but we always called it 'Nun's Trod.'

I was too young for punk but dimly remember older kids with docs and mohicans hanging out there and I had my first smoke down this alleyway when cornered by a group of boys. It was a stand off. They were wondering what to do. One of them had a cigarette and I asked him for a puff.

'You don't smoke,' he sneered.

'I want to,' I said. I held my ground, he handed it over. Crisis averted. By the time I was in the fifth form I was having a breakfast fag on the way to school.

We came out on to the main road again, next to the Catholic church. Matty and I went to Midnight Mass there, probably the last year we lived in Carlton when we were old enough to be out late on our own, but not yet allowed out to pubs and parties. I was surprised by the memory, as it seemed more my sort of thing to do than his. He was always firmly atheist and once got into trouble for a big argument with an RE teacher who believed in the literal truth of the Bible.

We looked at the gravestones. Some are people I knew or names I recognise and it's the same at the graveyard further up the road.

The two schools are at the outskirts of the village, just before you go over the bridge and either turn off for Drax or go straight on to Camblesforth – always known as Cammy.

I have few fond memories of my primary school where I continually felt like an outsider and thought the teachers were horrible to me. Luckily for me, I was so interested in books that not enjoying school didn't mean I didn't learn. Perhaps my intelligence was part of the problem. All my early teachers in Yorkshire seemed cross that I could read and write better than everyone else. When I first arrived, my teacher didn't believe I'd already read all the reading scheme books so made me start again. They were always making me read books again because I couldn't possibly have read them properly the first time. When we were asked what we wanted to do when we grew up, I'd say I wanted to be a detective or an author – I'd been reading Enid Blyton – and this was always derided.

I still remember the shame of being left out of the rounders team. The sheet was pinned up on the wall and we all gathered around to see what position we'd been picked for. Shame coursed through my body as my eyes flicked from post to post not seeing my name.

It was a small school and they'd put girls on the team who could hardly catch. Even at this distance and with a liking for giving people the benefit of the doubt, I can see no reason for my omission other than to punish me for being too big for my boots. Things got better in the last couple of years, with teachers who didn't seem to hate me for being an outsider and top of the class, and as escape to the big school next door got ever nearer.

The school fields joined each other. We walked past the shinty pitch. We had to wear black leotards for PE and I had obvious breasts from quite an early age which were much commented upon.

'You've already got tits.'

'Urghhh, You're DEVELOPING.'

I hated it and longed to be one of the slim flat-chested girls, though they didn't enjoy being called ironing boards. I was also suffering from the indignity of getting spots before anyone else. My nickname in my last year of primary school was Spot, and I've never been so relieved about anything as I was that it didn't transfer with me when I moved schools.

We reached the Holy Family, which still looks the same, a simple two storey block with a wooden cross on the wall. I wondered if it still smelt the same, of polish and incense. My parents weren't keen on sending us to a Catholic school. Neither of them liked religion, and my Dad had suffered a fair few whacks at the hands of the Christian Brothers when he was growing up, but nor did they want us to have to travel further so decided to make the best of it. I was excited about having a uniform and at the prospect of doing homework. My secondary school experience was much happier from the start. I had a delightful form teacher and I was made form captain. I loved all the new subjects, especially French, and it was fabulous to feel unleashed and to feel all my teachers valued my efforts.

I liked the religious stuff, too. We had Benediction every Thursday morning when a priest came in to swing a thurible in the air and bless us with incense. This was often further enlivened by one of the older girls fainting. Every few weeks there would be Mass on Thursday mornings and there was one glorious year when this clashed with double maths and I was thrilled to be missing my least favourite lesson. I read at Mass, but then I spoke whenever anything needed to be said and everyone would say how well spoken I was. I never worked out whether this was all to do with not having much of a Yorkshire accent, or whether I was just naturally good at speaking.

I was both eager to please and a bit rebellious, which I think was mainly about wanting to fit in. At that time, I was never a million miles away from being bullied at school for various reasons to do with being clever, having a posh voice, having an Irish father who went to the pub a lot, having a mother who went to work in a suit. I became adept at keeping in with all sides. I was top of the class and always wheeled out to meet the visiting dignitaries, but would then go off for a fag with the older boys. I taught myself to swear by practising in front of a mirror. 'Fuck off,' I'd say, watching myself to see if I could carry it off. 'Fuck off.' Later, when we started drinking, I had another way to make myself an asset as I could always get served because I looked old and was confident. This was a big deal and still contributes to the way I think of alcohol as a friend and resource, when I should be remembering that I no longer need to get served to have friends and, really, I could always be doing to have less of it.

In the second year I did metalwork and woodwork instead of housecraft like almost all the other girls, but the boys did all of my work for me. I think my mother still has the wooden pencil box almost entirely made by my friends Dale and Chris.

There were French exchange trips, skiing trips to Bulgaria, retreats in religious centres in North Leeds.

I was no longer any good at athletics after the second year, I had too much body to hurl into the long jump pit but I was good at netball and hockey. I was picked to play netball for the York and District team but by then I'd started to smoke and my interest in sport was waning.

We walked back along the main road past the Foresters, where my parents used to go for a drink and we'd sit in the children's room at the back with a bottle of coke and a bag of Roast Ox crisps. I liked it because there were loads of comics for girls like *Twinky* and *Bunty*, but Matty would get bored and want me to play with him instead of read. In the pub itself there was a big stuffed pike in a case.

Our friend Frank told me that shortly after my book came out he'd been in there playing darts and had overheard people talking about me at the bar.

'Cathy Mintern's written a book.'

'Has she?'

'Aye.'

'What's it about?'

'Dunno. But it's got people in it. From round here.'
'Has it?'

'Aye. She's got a different name now. Funny. Foreign.'

At which point Frank said, 'She's called Rentzenbrink.'

As we walked back out of the village I thought about how the two places, although divided only by a very short walk, felt so different to me. Despite lots of happy memories, Carlton is the place where we were outsiders, newcomers, never fully welcomed. When we moved to Snaith and moved into the pub, life took off.

I stopped on the bridge, poised between my two hometowns.

I looked down again at where I fell off the motorbike. There's a thing with memory, that when you write about it you become confused about what you can still remember and what you now know as words that you made and edited and have read aloud. Could I still feel the exhilaration before I fell off? Could I still smell the oil in the helmet? I caught a whiff of it. I tried to picture the scene below me. A girl falling off a bike, her brother and their dog running to see that she is OK.

My book has been optioned. If it does get turned into TV or film, and if they keep this scene in, then I might get to watch actors play us. If that happens, then my memory will be further overlaid and what remains of the original will dissipate into the air to join the other whispy ghosts of my previous selves and previous lives.

TALES FROM THE BELL & CROWN

OVER THE NEXT couple of days, I saw lots of old friends and the more I listened and talked, the more I felt my voice change. 'We're going to the Brewers Arms for something to eat and will be back in the Bell and Crown around eight' became 'We're off up to t' Brewers for summat to eat, we'll be back in t' Bell around eight.'

We ate well. You get big portions in Yorkshire and there's none of this trying to charge extra for vegetables. Erwyn, true to his Dutch identity of being thrifty, approved of more food for less money, though was perplexed by being served curry sauce with his fish and chips and tinned tomatoes with a fried breakfast. He was taken with the triangular black pudding we were given in the café next door that used to be a flower shop.

We drove around a bit, to Selby, Goole and

Doncaster. As we drove through Camblesforth I saw the Black Dog was up for sale. I always thought that was a good name for a pub. Some friends of mine used to chop down trees in the surrounding woods. £20 a day for back-breaking work in the freezing cold.

In Selby, we walked around the pubs and the Abbey and past the entrance of the China Palace, where we'd go for any sort of family celebration and also for the staff Christmas party. Prawn meat wrapped in rice paper was my favourite. I remembered a friend whose boyfriend lived in Selby. He split up with her because she wanted to go to university.

Back in Snaith, I didn't pull a pint or throw a dart, though I did hang out with the Ladies darts team one night and watch the men on the next. The men were playing on a Yorkshire board, which has no treble.

It was a delight to sit at the bar and laugh. The first night we went to bed at about 10.30 p.m. I lay there in the dark, listening to the sound of the jukebox still playing below. That's the thing about living above a pub. You are always aware that life is happening beneath you. You can hear the jukebox and occasional bursts of laughter. Back when we lived here, long before the smoking ban, you could smell upstairs when the first customer of the day lit up. Drew must be in, I'd think, and pop down to say hello. I loved this element of pub life; you didn't have to go far to find a friend or a bit of chat. I'd just walk downstairs and there would be someone around I'd enjoy talking to.

The Bell and Crown came up for sale when I was sixteen, the same time as Dad was feeling a bit old to be working shifts and spending large chunks of his life underground. He'd had another recent close shave at work when his leg had got tangled up in an airline and he'd been left dangling upside down in the shaft holding on tight and hoping that whoever had put it together had done a good job on the clamps. He thought he might finally have used up his nine lives. It was Matty who found out the pub was for sale and suggested we buy it. My parents had always been good savers and they managed to borrow the rest of the money they needed from breweries and the bank.

Moving in was exciting. Everyone wanted to help us and there was so much to explore. We'd been in the pub at night before, when it was packed with people, but I loved the way it felt to be there in the morning, the doors still closed to the outside world, knowing we were seeing the secrets of backstage. I was fascinated by the cellar, which was the oldest bit of the building, dark despite the electric light and with low ceilings that showed it dated from a time when people were shorter. There was a temperature controlled room that housed the beer barrels and then other rooms full of crates. There was a big trap door in the side alley through which the draymen would deliver. Now they came in lorries, but I liked to think back to the time when the cart would have been horse drawn and imagine the people who lived and worked in the pub then. The cellar was so atmospheric that I could almost hear whispers from the past when I was down there. I rather longed to meet a friendly ghost but it never happened. I did once, as I revisited in my dream, walk into a brace of pheasants, hung up in the cellar by one of our customers who'd had more to drink than planned and had forgotten they were there.

We both worked behind the bar at weekends and Matty bottled up every morning, fetching up replacements for all the bottles that had been drunk the night before. I loved chatting to the customers and playing darts and dominoes with them. My ears and eyes were out on stalks the whole time for all the interesting things they said.

Saturday afternoons were busy. Men would come in to watch horse racing on the telly and then play dominoes. One early evening, a man called Derek who'd been in all day wobbled up to the bar holding out a handful of change. 'How much for a G&T?' he said. I told him and, after much staring down at the coins in his hand, he said, 'And how much just for the G?'

There was a small holder who would bring my dad courgettes in exchange for a couple of pints and who proposed to me one day. I felt like I was in a DH Lawrence novel. 'I could get a record player for you, lass' he said, when I declined. It became a habit and he proposed to me every time he came in. When I realised I hadn't seen him for a while I wondered if he'd taken his heart and his courgettes elsewhere and I hoped he'd found a nice girl who was enjoying the record player.

We loved the jukebox and the great thrill of being empowered to take 50p out of the till to hand to a customer when it was quiet so they could put some tunes on. I'd always try to give it to people I knew didn't have much money. I remember Madonna, Simply Red and Soul II Soul playing all the time when we moved in. If I was choosing songs myself, I'd pick The Cure and Soft Cell and Bowie. The opening bars of 'Queen Bitch' still have the power to transport me right back there, to the front room of the pub, next to the pool table.

When I lived in France a few years later, I came home to find that Brit Pop had happened and 'Common People' by Pulp was the song of that summer. I'd been living in Normandy near the D-Day beaches and had brought back a postcard of Arromanches and its mulberry harbours for one of our customers who used to come in for two halves on pension day and had fought at what he called 'Arrowmanchess.' Of course, I never corrected his pronunciation but I was interested that the soldiers had never learnt to say the names of the places they were liberating.

It wasn't all rosy and I had to develop a thicker skin. Whenever the phone rang at the pub, various men would say, 'Tell her I'm not here,' and I'd have to lie on their behalf. I remember once hearing one man saying to another, 'I'm not having some split-arse telling me what to do.' It took me a while to work out what he meant and I was a bit scared both by the ugliness of the expression and by the menace in his voice.

If you took offence at anyone, they'd say, 'Oh, Barnsley playing at home, are they?' or, even more bluntly, 'What's up with you? Are you on t'rag?'

I didn't know what to do about this at first but got good at just fixing someone with a stare and saying, 'Oh, fuck off.'

There was a joke about why you shouldn't trust a woman: you can't trust anything that bleeds for seven days and doesn't die.

One day, I was standing in a large circle of people opposite a man called Gary, a big brute of a man who prided himself on his physical strength. He'd told me he'd been in the SAS. Someone else later told me that wasn't true. Perhaps he'd been in the Territorial Army for a bit. I said something – I can't now remember what but I think I made a joke at his expense. He stared at me from across the circle of people and said, 'You need to learn to shut your mouth.' I remember the shock I felt at the violence of this and the hot blush of red all the way up to the roots of my hair. I knew that it was for me to make things right, that I would have to apologise and charm him, which I managed to do. He became a friend of sorts, in that way you are friends with people who come in your pub because you don't have much choice about it. I never liked him very much and thought he was a bit of a liar. Later, I found out that he had made up a story that he had had sex with me, that he'd shagged me over our pool table. It was such a feeble and obvious fantasy that it never much bothered me, but I still think about him telling me I needed to learn to shut my mouth.

My father gloried in my conversation, was fiercely proud that I was, as he'd often say, lots cleverer than him, but that wasn't the way Yorkshire men tended to think about their women. And no one liked an attention seeker. The thing in Yorkshire was to not show yourself up, not be too full of yourself. I spent large chunks of my life trying not to be too clever or too strange. You're full of yourself, people would say, not as a compliment, or, you like the sound of your own voice. You didn't want to be too big for your boots, so sharp you'd cut yourself, or sound as though you'd swallowed a dictionary. Book learning won't get you a husband, I was told. You don't want to be left on the shelf.

I never minded Frank saying I was so sharp I'd cut myself, as he always did it with a wry smile. He used to tell my dad I would never settle down and marry a man from around here and that I would have to go off to bigger places, all of which, of course, turned out to be true.

I've lived in lots of places, all of which have shaped

me, as have the people I've known and the jobs I've done. Now my life is taking a different turn because I forced myself to write my first book. Some people liked it and that has emboldened me to try to live as a writer. My long ago ambition. There is another version of me who decided to give up on those silly dreams, who decided to put the notebooks away and focus on work. That person is probably more competent. I find that indulging my creative brain takes a toll on my ability to move around the world in an effective way. When I've been writing fiction I can hardly trust myself to get on a bus or try to cook a pot of soup. I end up in the wrong places. I burn things. I get confused about what is true, what is made up and what I've dreamt or read about. I worry I'll unintentionally plagiarise someone because I'll have grafted their words on to my own unruly thought tree and can no longer tell which branch belongs to whom.

I could be gloriously impractical in Snaith because people were always around to bail me out. Once I fused all the upstairs electrics by trying to cook a steak in the toaster when drunk and someone sorted it out. Everyone thought it was hilarious and, a couple of weeks later, when Ricky thought about trying to cook a pork chop in the toaster in *Eastenders*, we all wondered if the story had spread far and wide.

'Have you put any oil in that car of yours, yet?' men would ask, over the bar.

'Do I have to?' I'd say, and everyone would laugh and someone would do it for me.

I learnt so much from working in the pub, above all tolerance of others and excellent radar. These days, I like to try to be trusting because I think people who are too cynical miss out. I'd rather be duped every so often than exhaust myself by living from a place of suspicion. Having said all that, I know that part of being able to take that attitude is because the pub taught me excellent radar. My instincts about people were honed and sharpened. I have a good nose for truth and lies, a good sense about whether or not a new person is going to turn out to be too good to be true. I know when people are annoying but harmless, and I know when a fight is about to break out. In the pub, I not only knew who was having an affair with whom, but could often see it coming before the people involved did. I also learnt discretion. My dad often said that he felt like a father confessor because everyone told him their secrets. I learnt both to listen to secrets and to keep them to myself. I learnt a profound truth that I still think about all the time: you never know the size of someone else's paper round, and it is safer and kinder to assume that everyone has a cross to bear.

Of course, people would be mean and rude and I had to be able to carry on doing my job. I couldn't show weakness. These days I think it is OK to be a bit vulnerable, but behind a bar on a busy night isn't the place for it.

Sometimes the undercurrents tipped into actual violence and I'll never forget the first time I saw someone glassed in the face. I got good at knowing what could be smoothed over, what had the potential to erupt, when the police needed to be called. Boxing Day was always a bit of a tinder box as people had been spending too much time cooped up with their families and could only bite their tongues for so long. Often a long fermenting family quarrel would explode under our noses.

Now, I feel all this gave me a sense of perspective. During my first Christmas as a bookseller, when others were complaining about working Christmas Eve, I'd think, well, at least most of our customers will not be drunk, we get to go home at 5 p.m., and there is zero chance that come midnight I'll be standing in the main street with no glass left in our front windows and covered in someone else's blood.

There are lessons in resilience to be had too, and in not taking things too seriously. Running a pub is a bit like writing a book in that you have to do your best and not water your beer, but there will always be someone who doesn't like it and you have to not care too much about that.

I've often amused festival goers by telling them that chairing literary events uses the same skills as running a busy bar – you need to be interested in people and stories and to enjoy making sure everybody has a good time. You also need to maintain good order over your crowd, whether they are queuing for drinks or putting their hands up to ask a question. In the same way that you shouldn't just serve one section of the bar and ignore the people waiting on the other side, you shouldn't just take questions from people sitting at the front of the auditorium and ignore those at the back. If someone is too drunk or too angry, they need to leave the pub because they are ruining it for everyone else. If someone tries to turn asking an author a question into recounting a long story about themselves and the manuscript that is a masterpiece that they happen to have with them, then they need to be gently cut off because there are plenty of other people whose right to have a good time must be respected.

And there are stories galore. My friend Kaye reminded me that I was always saying that I'd write a book one day, and that when people asked me if they'd be in it, I'd say, well, if you are, you won't recognise yourself.

I miss the pub when things go wrong, when I feel vulnerable. Recently when Erwyn and Matt were both ill, and I only had one bucket and I had to work out which of them was most likely to be sick next, I thought how if I was living above the pub in Snaith, there would be no shortage of people who would come round and help me. Life would be full of friends who would bring me buckets, make me cups of tea, tidy and cheer me up.

Though, on the other side of the scales, you have enough of being observed and discussed. I remember when I was moving to London, everyone kept telling me that they'd heard people in London didn't know their neighbours. Yes, I'd think. I can't wait. I was fed up of everyone speculating over my boyfriends and my behaviour. I was younger then. Now I value the sense of community more.

What do I take from Yorkshire now? I'm aware that 'Yorkshire' to me means something entirely personal and subjective. It describes not a place but a collection of experiences. When I hear the word I think of my parents and my brother, of alleyways and snickets and pubs, of power stations and netball courts and dartboards. It means childhood and coming of age. It means tragedy more than recovery. It remains the place where sad things happened, though it is also the place that furnished huge support and friendship. And still does. On my recent visit I felt very happy sitting at the bar in the Bell and Crown with my old friends. They asked if I could imagine living there now and, in some ways, I could. I think it would be good for me to be surrounded by people who say what they think, who are rooted in the earth. Part of me craves to know where I am. 'I speak as I find,' a Yorkshire person will say, leaving you in no doubt of their opinion. 'You always did think too much,' says another friend, which makes me laugh and long to spend more time surrounded by people who would help me keep my feet on the ground. I would feel more solid if I came back to live in Yorkshire. More sure-footed among these people who know who they are.

I feel grateful to it and can see that I need to re-connect to my Yorkshire barmaid self, to that girl who, yes, blushed when told to shut her mouth, but who stayed in the room and didn't run away. I didn't shut my mouth and I didn't care about stories of being shagged over the pool table. I can't imagine that girl wasting her time fretting about horrible reviews, spiteful comments or indeed anything at all. I need to channel her.

I was telling my friend Jase that I found it difficult when people were mean about me or my book and he looked at me as though I was insane. 'You've become a right Southern softie,' he said. 'What you do, if someone is funny with you, is you just think "Fuck 'em."'

And this is where Matty comes in, my dear lost brother; whenever I imagine what he would think of it all, I see the massive eyebrow raise he would deliver to me for the fact that I care about anyone's negative opinion. He just wouldn't understand it. 'Fuck that,' he'd say. 'Why are you caring about that? Why are you caring about what those non-entities think about you?'

Matty had more of a Yorkshire accent than I did and lived a far greater percentage of his life there because, of course, he never got to move away and do other things. My mother loves maps and surrounds herself with them so the bungalow had maps all over the walls, and even their duvet cover was a map of the world. I remember sitting by Matty as he was dying thinking how unfair it was that he would never get to go to new places, that all his intelligence and wanderlust and curiosity had come to such a terrible end. If he'd died on the night he was knocked over, then he would have been cremated the week afterwards and we'd have scattered his ashes somewhere in Yorkshire. Around Carlton ponds maybe, where we used to collect conkers or in the back fields where we used to play. Or maybe in the river under Snaith and Carlton Bridge, just by where we used to walk Polly. There would have been floral tributes tied into the hedges by the bit of road where he took his last breath with a fully working brain. We would have been distraught and bereft but I don't think we'd have been damaged in the same relentless way that we were by his eight years of non-life and by having to decide that he should die. Though, finally, through writing my book and talking to other people who have experienced a similar loss I am able to see Matty's death as an act of love. It wasn't the last one, as it turned out, because I now see that the real last act of love we can do for the people who leave us is to try to live well without them.

Matty exists in people's memories in Yorkshire. He has a physical footprint here and I love that I am surrounded by people who knew him, that I bump into the lovely woman who was walking next to him the night he was knocked over, that they are still giving out the Matthew Mintern Award for Achievement up at his school, that it is now being won by the children of his friends. His friend, our friend, Ian sent me a message on Matty's birthday as he was about to sit down with a large glass of red wine and have his own little annual remembrance.

The day after we got back from Yorkshire I woke up with a tune on my lips, 'Electric Dreams' by The Human League. I hadn't thought of or heard this song for years. I spend the day humming it, not remembering the words, beyond the title and always being together. So, I looked it up and the second verse seemed so utterly relevant to my situation and how I now need to think about my dear lost brother, which is about the gifts that I had from his friendship and that he did teach me to be brave. And that is what

Yorkshire gave, it provided a haven for this family who were on the move, it hosted us for a while.

My brother shared my heritage. I feel lonely without him, though I've learnt to feel lucky that I had a partner in crime for sixteen years, rather than only focus on what I lost. What happened to him shaped me – I've gone for a neutral word there but I'm more drawn towards a word like maimed or damaged or thwarted – but so did my childhood. One of the things I feel very lucky about is my relationship with men. I love men and don't fear them. I think of them as friends and comrades. And it's not that I haven't ever been frightened or badly treated by a man, but no individual incident has ever dinted the overall joy I feel in their company that is the gift of growing up with a good father and a good brother. My dad, my brother and his friends, and then the customers of our pub fitted me for a lifetime's worth of enjoying male friendship. The pub also taught me how to navigate less friendly territory, and that is also something to be thankful for. The world is an imperfect place but I do know how to move through it safely. Rather than fret about the fact that I don't feel I fit in anywhere, I should celebrate it. Where am I from? Lots of places. I can pick and choose.

The sense of otherness is a gift, of a sort. Writers come in all different shapes and sizes but if they have one thing in common it's that they are outsiders. My lack of belonging is a liberation. If I identified more with a place or a people, I might be even more frightened of writing about it. You need distance and not to be too invested.

I don't need to learn to shut my mouth, but I do need to try to care less about what happens when I open it. I need to be full of myself, so full of myself that stories and words burst out of me. Yes, I am sharp, but I won't cut myself. Yes, I do like the sound of my own voice. Yes, I have not only swallowed a dictionary but I have chewed on every word as it went down. And when people don't like what I do, I need to channel my Yorkshire barmaid self and those wise, kind Yorkshire friends who have a way of cutting through the crap to deliver robust chunks of wisdom, and I need to think 'Fuck 'em.' And that is good advice for anyone.

Yorkshire has been revisited and reclaimed. Last night I went to the Bell and Crown again. I sat at the bar with old friends and we laughed and joked and talked about what we love and what we fear and I felt at home. Home is people, really, far more than it is places or buildings. For as long as I have friends in Snaith who remember me as the girl from the Bell and Crown then a little bit of me will always belong there.

The Island upon the Moor

Victoria Hennison

VICTORIA HENNISON was born in Yorkshire and still lives in the county today, in a small village with her husband and children.

WHEN I THINK about home, the image that arises in my mind is of a medieval church on an isolated hill with fields and marshland spreading out as far as the eye can see. This is Holme-upon-Spalding-Moor – known by its friends as Holme or H.O.S.M – the island upon the moor. Or rather, this is how Holme might have first appeared when it came into being in the thirteenth century: a residential plain built on the holme around a church. I say might, as some believe that the village and the church were once on a level plain, but as the marshlands were drained the village sank lower, leaving the church standing proud on a hill of Keuper marl – layers of red mudstone and siltstone. I like the landscape – the single hill and ancient church, its most prominent feature.

The village is now one of the largest in the East Riding of Yorkshire. Located on the edge of the

Yorkshire Wolds, it isn't especially hilly or indeed rugged as the Moors are in the north of the county. Over the centuries, the marsh has transformed into farmland, and the village was briefly known as Hemp Holme in the eighteenth century when much of the land was used for the cultivation of hemp. In 1823, the *Baines History, Directory and Gazetteer* listed twenty-three farmers as belonging to the village – other occupations included blacksmiths, wheelwrights and shoemakers – and farming remains a key industry today, with many of the farms passing down through the generations, bringing welcome continuity in times of growth and change.

I moved to the village in 1984 when I was two years old. It was just the three of us – my mum, my brother and me. I always thought of us as the three musketeers. It was us against the world. Holme is the only place I can remember living as a child but while it feels as though I spent my entire childhood there, Mum tells me there were two villages before Holme, equally small, unknown gems in the Yorkshire countryside: Birdsall and Broughton. I am a Yorkshire lass born and bred.

Today the village consists of a long wide road with a maze of public footpaths, lanes and quiet residential streets drifting off from it. There is a traditional post office, a red telephone box, a village hall and several cosy pubs. But it has grown quickly in the last twenty years, and when I go back now, it seems more like a town than a village – with a wide spread of new brick houses, shops and takeaways mingling with the old stone cottages.

But I think it retains the same traditional values and community spirit that have made it both my friend and enemy over the years: safe and fun when I was little and then increasingly claustrophobic as I became a teenager. When I slipped into a period of dark depression, the village became more than a backdrop. It provided solace and quiet at a time of deep pain, when the only relief I could find was by cutting into my own skin. I think we all have a beautiful place in our minds, a home we can return to during difficult times. And even though I have now made my life somewhere else – close by, in another Yorkshire village – I still treasure the winding roads, ploughed fields and a view of the sun setting behind the church. Holme-upon-Spalding-Moor will always be meaningful to me. Childhood memories and nostalgia keep it in my heart.

I REMEMBER MY early years growing up in Holme-upon-Spalding-Moor as idyllic. Our family home was a three-bed semi on a quiet street in the village: a pretty house with a fenced garden and roses leading to the door. Mum was a keen gardener and there wasn't a weed to be seen or a petal out of place. My mum got her green fingers from her father, my grandad. He passed away before I was born, but many of the shrubs that grew in our garden came from seedlings and buds that he himself had cultivated. My mum simply dug them up and moved them wherever she went.

My father, a police sergeant in North Yorkshire, left when I was a baby, but he was never absent from my life, and though he worked long hours and his shifts varied, I regularly spent weekends with him in the police house he occupied in the village of Pateley

Bridge. It was the kind of house you draw as a child, a huge stone structure with a big wooden door, an iron knocker and brass doorknob. The police quarters were behind a locked door, and on the rare occasions I ventured through, I can remember slipping and sliding across the polished marble floor in my socks towards the grand wooden desk at the end of the corridor. I knew I shouldn't have disturbed him while he was working, but I don't think he minded really. When he came in late from work, he would always kiss me good night, his moustache tickling my cheek.

I had a wonderful childhood. Every child in the village felt like a friend, but there was one girl in particular who I thought of as my best friend. To play after school I would ride my bike through the fields that lay behind my house, taking a snicket we called the 'curly wurly' – a twisty dirt track that led to her home. We were inseparable. Her dad, prompted by the fact we were born only a few days' apart and possessed equally mischievous ways, nicknamed us the terrible twins.

There was another special girl, slightly older than me, who lived next door. She was like a big sister and tied ribbons in my hair while we played with my dolls and little plastic kitchen. I see photos of my younger self now: blue eyes, blonde curls and pinafore dresses, and wonder whether I seemed like a doll to her. At least I knew she would never cut off my hair, unlike my big brother who thought it would be funny to shear my Sindy, poor thing.

As I grew up and swapped dresses for jeans, I was thought of as a tomboy. I enjoyed kicking about in the Yorkshire mud, building dens and climbing trees, or taking carrots to feed the horses in the field. So much of life was dictated by the seasons. In the summer, we would leave the house early in the morning and not come back until sunset, occasionally grabbing a snack as we sped through. Armed with water pistols, we'd run and hide, preparing to soak any unsuspecting victim: 'Ha ha, I am going to get you' – the warning call – 'not if I catch you first' – the beastly reply.

We rode our bikes for miles along the old railway line, through the greenery, away from the traffic and the people on the high street. Holme Moor railway closed to passengers in 1954 and then completely in 1965, so I have only ever known it as a disused line, although I have seen photos of the station in its heyday. The main building had a bay window overlooking the platform and there was a booking office and a timber waiting shelter. I used to enjoy standing at one end of the village and staring down the long wildlife corridor, picturing a train chugging towards me from the other end. I remember thinking I could jump on that train and it would take me anywhere I wished – to find One-Eyed Willy's treasure, a secret garden or the doorway to Narnia. I was prepared to cling on and hope I would enjoy the final destination.

If we weren't riding our bikes, we were probably playing blockie, a game that is a cross between hide-and-seek and British Bulldog. I'm not sure if it's a Yorkshire game or something we made up, but someone would shout 'block 1, 2, 3,' as he or she reached the target area, which would attract the attention of the seeker, and then we would all charge at once. It was harder to be caught if we went as one. A gang of us climbed trees, and I was an expert, climbing to the highest branch and sitting there with my legs dangling, encouraging everyone to come join me in the clouds where we could dream of adventures and spot faraway secret lands.

No one locked their doors then. I was welcomed into the homes of friends and neighbours without question. As children, we certainly didn't worry about crime or being unsafe in the world. We had no sense of danger. When we played in the old quarry, we would slide down the embankment to the bottom and try to grab hold of tree branches to guide us along the slick muddy sides of the pit. We would swing from trees, kicking off from the ground and dangling in the air, then letting go and splashing into the small lake at the bottom.

Our final summer days, those last years of primary school, were the best. Springfield – an area of waste ground – was one of our favourite haunts. I remember hiding in the long grass, climbing up piles of stone and clambering into an old rusty digger to share snacks and tell stories. A few tall trees surrounded the boggy swamp. The earth was always saturated with water – as black as tar – and nothing grew there. Everything just sank – leaves, sticks, a toy boat one of the boys brought along once – all sucked beneath the surface of this black lagoon. Legend has it that a horse and cart came riding through the village one night, took a wrong turn off the track and became stuck in the swamp. Unable to escape, the horse, cart and its passengers are said to have sunk to the depths of the abyss, pulled under by the power of the swamp, never to be found.

I would often go to spend part of the school holidays with my dad's parents – my grandma and grandad – in Harrogate, where they ran a kennel and guard dog security firm. Their house stood in the centre of large grounds, with trees all around which were great for climbing. Grandma called out to me one time: 'Get down before you fall down'. They had goats, dogs, cats and rabbits – it was a fantastic place to be. My grandad was a typical Yorkshireman. He wore a flat cap and a tweed jacket and didn't mince his words: he called a spade a spade. He treated me like a princess, of course. I adored him and my grandma too. I loved spending time with them and was spoilt rotten.

*

I enjoyed all the village festivities growing up. Year after year, they were always the same and I had no reason to believe anything would ever change.

My mum and I would wander the stalls of the annual summer gala, trying our luck on the tombola, while my brother, who was several years older and far too cool to come with us, went round with his friends. If we were lucky, he'd give us a cheeky wink in acknowledgement from afar. He was a typical big brother: he'd buy me penny sweets from the shop and push me on the swings at the park while also playing tricks on me and winding me up something rotten. I wouldn't have him any other way though, and I gave as good as I got!

After the summer gala, we could watch for the arrival of the travelling fair – the huge trucks and trailers folding open to reveal the rides. I remember spinning on the waltzers until I felt sick, trying to hook a duck, goldfish in plastic bags, motorbikes whizzing round the speedway, plus trying my luck on the arcade machines and penny slots ...

I loved Halloween when the streets filled with children wearing costumes and painted faces, witches' hats and devils' horns, vampire teeth and capes. I knew which doors would be answered and which would ignore the knocking, and I even knew what I'd get at certain houses, from certain people, like the little old lady who always gave pennies bagged into one pound's worth from a big stash of copper she'd gathered throughout the year. There was the house with the grumpy old man whose door I'd never dare knock on. And another man who always asked for a trick because he thought himself funny. I'd shrug and eventually he'd concede defeat, pulling a bowl of sweets from behind his back.

For bonfire night we would stand in a muddy field

underneath the night sky in the grounds of Holme
Hall, a grade II listed eighteenth-century building
serving as a Sue Ryder care home. Huddled together
in our warm coats, scarves, mittens and wellies, we'd
kick up the autumn leaves and slosh our way through
the mud, our feet becoming filthier with every step.
I loved breathing in the smoky sulphur of used
sparklers and the warm meaty smell of the hot dogs.
Clutching one wrapped in a napkin and topped with
fried onions, I'd join my mum in the crowd by the
fire.

It was a huge spectacle with bright yellow flames
and orange embers that burned as hot as lava. I used
to imagine it was a fire dragon roaring with fury and
spitting charcoal. In the middle stood Guy Fawkes,
usually stuffed with wool and wearing a tatty blazer.
His eyes would be painted red and, pinned to a big
brown stick, he looked like a demon glaring down at
me. I watched spellbound as logs were tossed onto
the beautiful blaze and the heat became more intense.
The crowd was silent as the fireworks started with
a crackle and pop before the rockets illuminated the
night sky. Then the little children would scream with
delight and sometimes with fear, their yelps piercing
through my eardrums, as the fireworks exploded

– neon colours and glitter thrown against the black sky, like paint being flicked onto a canvas. Although I didn't know it then, my life would be just like those fireworks, bright sparks of colour and light and then a blanket of darkness.

Winters in our village were magical. I'd look forward to the ice freezing over the Springfield swamp so I could glide across it in my boots, pretending to be an ice skater. And when it snowed and Church Hill was a long white plane, we'd swarm there with sledges and plastic sacks, gasping for breath as we slipped and slid and rolled our way down. Sledging down was such a thrill, although the walk back up was not so much fun. We could spend hours there, until our fingers and toes lost all feeling, and then it was time to head home to warm up in front of the coal fire.

And of course Christmas was the best thing about those winter months. A real tree standing in the corner of the room, its plant pot wrapped in red tissue paper and paper chains draped across the ceiling. The excitement of the old cardboard box appearing from the loft, all the decorations individually wrapped inside, and at the very bottom, another box with separated compartments containing beautiful sparkly ornaments made of glass. Hidden amongst those ornaments on the tree were cardboard egg cups wrapped in tin foil and fairies made out of paper plates – decorations my brother and I lovingly made and my mum lovingly kept and still brings out to this day. 'The most precious decorations of all,' she says.

Whatever the season or holiday, Sundays were family days and if I went out with my friends, I would always return for lunch. Roast beef and Yorkshire puddings, roast potatoes, lashings of gravy and a few vegetables on the side, followed by a home-made apple crumble with custard. It was tradition – the one meal of the week that we'd sit down as a family to eat. The television was always switched off, and instead Mum would put the radio on or set a record spinning on the turntable. Elvis Presley or Jim Reeves were her favourites, but she had a vast selection of LPs. In the summer, we were allowed out again after dinner to play in the afternoon. The ice cream van would come a-calling at some point and as soon as we heard the familiar jingle, no matter how full our bellies were, we'd split off and run home begging for a pound. I'm sure every parent groaned as they heard the music tinkling down the street, but most gave in and we would all sit together on the wall by the football pavilion enjoying ice cream dribbled with raspberry sauce. Those who were really lucky, or had been especially good, were treated to a flake. I always had a tub rather than a cornet, so I could swirl the sauce and make raspberry ripple.

*

I enjoyed primary school. It was a small community – ten classrooms, an assembly hall, cloakrooms and toilets – with a nursery within the grounds, some lush green lawns and flowers beds. There was a huge clock at the front of the school with a stone that dated it back to 1875. Although there have been extensions and additions over the years, the original building still stands, and I am not sure it has changed all that much.

I can remember each classroom and each teacher, even though I wasn't taught by all of them. Everyone was so kind and friendly: the headmaster with his office under the spiral staircase, the school secretary who always welcomed me with a smile. It was that kind of place. Safe and secure. I had moved up from the nursery and recognised every face in the playground. We had fun and caused mischief of course, but I loved my lessons too, especially those that allowed me to write stories and draw pictures, to set my imagination free.

The day started with assembly, which involved hymns and the Lord's Prayer displayed via the overhead projector, the acetate often upside down. Then we'd sit in our lessons, watching the hands of the clock tick by, waiting for the bell to sound in the hallway, a signal that it was time to play or for lunch. School dinners were the best. Oh the excitement of pink custard dripping over chocolate concrete! As the bell rang for playtime, I – along with children in the other classes – would charge out through the doors, eager to be outside. There were several doors opening into the playground so it would be quite an explosion. At break we played a variety of games: hopscotch, skipping, or leapfrog on the tyres. We also had a sand tunnel – basically a concrete builder's tunnel on a hill that was surrounded by sand. The girls would spend hours sweeping the sand out and the mean boys would kick it all back in. I would balance on the wall and hope the bell wouldn't ring too soon.

*

In such a close community, no one was a stranger. Everyone in the village seemed to know when it was your birthday and everyone was invited to the party. To leave a child out would have been unfair.

My parties were the same every year: smiling faces, balloons and cake. Girls were dropped off in party dresses and boys in jeans and freshly-ironed T-shirts, all holding cards and presents. We ate sandwiches, sausage rolls and cocktail sausages on sticks, party rings, chocolate fingers and Tunnock's tea cakes. My mum always made a small rabbit jelly just for me and a larger rabbit blancmange for the table. I can't actually remember anyone eating the blancmange, but it was tradition. We'd play pass the parcel and musical chairs, with pop tunes blaring out on cassette tape, and then it was time to cut the cake. Mum used to bring it in with the candles lit and all the guests would sing 'Happy Birthday' as I blew them out.

I think part of the reason I loved my birthday was because I wanted to grow up. I can recall an old chap once shouting at a group of us as we rode our bikes through the village, 'Enjoy that freedom, it doesn't last!' But we thought adult life would bring more freedoms – the chance to come and go as we pleased, answerable to no one.

And it's true, we sought out risk and adventure. I can remember playing in an old derelict barn, tying a rope to the rafters to create a swing and lighting a fire, ignoring the warning signs about unsafe buildings and fragile roofs. It was crumbling before our eyes: the ground was covered in a blanket of dust and splinters and there were big holes in the roof. We used to pass the hours whittling sticks and playing sword fights. 'Do you ever dream about being famous,' a boy asked me once. 'Nah, I want to write stories,' I told him. 'To escape from reality and hide in the pages . . .' He grinned. 'You're good at telling stories. I want to be in a band.' He strummed wildly, playing air guitar until we all laughed and joined in, jumping around, pretending we were rock stars.

*

But by the time I was eleven, I was starting to feel a little unsettled. The girl who had been my best friend up to that point moved away and although I had other friends I missed my 'twin'. We kept in touch by writing letters and sleeping over at each other's houses, but it wasn't the same. She felt a million miles away. Secondary school was looming and this meant lots of new people. I was comfortable with my village friends, but painfully shy with those I didn't know, and new situations did not sit at all well with me. The more I pondered the change, the more I worried about it.

During that last year of primary school, I started to disappear as soon as I had arrived home and changed out of my uniform. I had fashioned a hiding place in a tiny corner of a field where the trees and bushes had become overgrown. My only companions were the few birds nestled in the trees above. Lying in the grass, daydreaming, or simply listening to the leaves dance in the breeze like musical notes in a song, gave me some relief. I could run or skip or sing or cry undisturbed. I felt as if I were part of nature, as if I truly belonged.

As I feared, starting secondary school was really hard. I went from a small village school where I knew everyone to a much larger secondary school in the town of Market Weighton; from a class of fewer than thirty to a year of over one hundred. Children came from all the surrounding villages and it felt as though I were adrift in a sea of strangers with only a handful of old faces dotted throughout. I felt a little better when I discovered that my best friend would be joining me (she really hadn't gone too far away) and when my brother, who was in his final year, occasionally gave me a thumbs up when we passed in the corridor. But slowly everyone seemed to separate off as new friendships and cliques were formed. I found myself the odd one out and became lonely for the first time in my life.

The girls were all generally friendly in class but there was a group who teased me, away from prying eyes and listening ears. It battered my confidence when they'd say things like, 'no one likes you.' The bus ride to and from school became the hardest part of the day once my brother had left. A few older boys would throw their school bags at me and goad me as I tried to ignore them: 'She'll never say anything; she doesn't speak.' I felt that it must somehow be my fault, that I didn't really fit in or belong anywhere.

Looking back, this struggle to fit in was the beginning of a dark period. I noticed the absence of a label keenly. I wasn't the popular girl, the nerd or the geek, the loner, the goth, the goody two shoes or the rebel. I wasn't the brightest or the dumbest. At a time when feeling special mattered so very much, I felt average and ordinary – a blank page without words or colour.

At first I tried to blend in and was so grateful our school had a uniform so I could look the same as everyone else. The need to impress people on non-uniform days was torture – there was so much pressure to have an image and to decide who I should be. Later, I dyed my blonde hair black and shrouded myself in black clothes, perhaps in an attempt to fade into the background, to disappear entirely. My jewellery was chunky with chains and studs, and my ears were full of piercings. I wanted everyone to keep their distance. No one batted an eyelid. I was just a teenager trying out new fads. There are very few photos of my early teenage years, as if the camera had broken, but I'd rather file those years under delete anyway. I didn't much like myself then.

I found that the village changed too. It seemed to shrink and there was less and less to do. The boys were suddenly too cool to hang out with the girls and the girls seemed to spend more time with friends from other villages – visiting their homes or going shopping after school. Holme is no man's land to everyone aged twelve to eighteen. We had outgrown our surroundings: too old for play and too young for the pub. I remember my mum saying, 'Only boring people get bored. If you're bored, I can find you something to do.' The words trip off my tongue now that I am a mother. But then the village felt like a place to escape from. I had barely been out of Yorkshire, but I longed to see more of the world. I started to dream about going to university and landing a good job, getting married, buying a house and having children. I assumed it would all fall into place one day and that any irrational feelings would disappear.

But for a time during my teens life just did not make sense; there was this shadow that clung to me and got bigger and bigger until it consumed me completely. I drew myself away from friends – my narrow circle narrowing further – and my family. I felt that I couldn't talk to anyone. I didn't live up to social expectations and no matter how hard I tried I was probably pretty impossible to be around. I couldn't give any explanations for my behaviour or my attitude. Understandably, my friends lost patience – my life appeared no different to theirs and they couldn't see why I was so down. In the end they walked away.

My life seemed to become a little easier when people stopped trying to figure me out, but ultimately isolation sent me on a downward spiral. I was thirteen years old when I first cut myself. It was tea time – our weekly Tuesday fish and chip supper, a treat as my mum always worked in the evening that day. As with every other week, my brother and I argued over who would go to collect the fish and chips, and as usual I insisted I would not give in but in the end was the one to get on my bike. On this particular day, I rode to the chippy and skidded along the curb, falling into the road, grazing my knee and cutting my elbow. It really hurt, but what sticks in my mind are the words the man behind the counter in the chip shop said as I walked in: 'Smile, it might never happen, duck.' The words were meant kindly but they struck me as cruel. It already had happened. I was in pain but shrugged and said nothing. Yorkshire folk are like that. They speak to anyone and everyone with a smile and a term of endearment: 'duck', 'chuck', 'petal'. Most of the time it's welcome but sometimes I'd prefer a little more thought, a little more distance.

I grabbed my bag of chips and cycled home, blood dripping down my arm and a strange sense of relief washing over me. It was odd, but I felt calm. I left my chips on the kitchen sideboard and went to my bedroom to sit and watch as the blood seeped into my shirt. I wanted the feeling of stillness to last a little longer, so I took an old broken compact mirror and removed a section from its casing. I pushed the silver shard into the cut, allowing the blood to flow more strongly. It was a form of control, a way to free myself from pain. I cried myself to sleep that night, looking out of the window at the stars and hoping never to wake up.

Cutting myself became a coping mechanism. I felt

invisible in the dark of my bedroom and would slice my skin with the mirrored shards, and all the hurt that I had buried inside would dissipate. I never used anything sharper; the thought of putting a knife to my skin made me shiver. I didn't want to harm myself, not really. I just wanted to see myself bleed; the tiniest of cuts would do it. They looked like the cuts and scrapes I could easily get from climbing a tree and scrambling over a wall. Not particularly noticeable. Nothing out of the ordinary. And I would just open old scars, rather than create new ones.

There were days when I felt fine. I could go to school and come home bright with laughter. But then there were days when my insecurities mounted up and I struggled to maintain any sort of calm. I can remember feeling totally overwhelmed, unable to stop crying or control my temper. I found the physical pain easier to bear than the inner turmoil. I knew that it seemed wrong and that no one would understand if I told them. I didn't want anyone to find out. I could imagine what they'd say – a list of reasons to be happy and things to be grateful for – but I didn't want their advice. I didn't want to be fixed.

The relief was temporary, of course, and the peace short-lived. I desperately wanted to feel the calm I had felt that first time on my bike. As time went on, I found simply pricking my finger with the sharp point of a pin would give me that feeling of relief, the sudden 'ow' and the bubble of blood. Sometimes I needed to repeat the action, but it felt easier to handle. It was no different to those kids threading their skin with sewing needles in textiles class, no bigger wound, no real harm. I could rationalise it if I had no wounds to hide, no need to make explanations as to why old scars hadn't yet healed. It was a ritual that kept me sane.

I'm not sure if anyone ever suspected anything. Maybe they did but were too kind to say, too embarrassed, or too worried about the consequences. I'm fairly certain my mum didn't know. We had a really good relationship and I respected her immensely. She worked all the hours she could while always managing to drop us off at school and pick us up. Every sports day, every parents' evening and every school play, she was always there. I never went without and I am so grateful to her. We were a single-parent family (not a label we wanted, but one we got anyway), but we were a happy family and I had the same love as everyone else. I never felt a need to rebel. I never went out and got horrifically drunk or took drugs.

There weren't many rules or boundaries, but there didn't need to be. I always felt that I had my mum's trust. I knew that she loved me and would always be there if ever I needed her. I came first. She is an amazing woman, one in a million, but somehow – as much as I wanted to snap out of my gloom for her – I just couldn't defeat it.

I tend to think of those days as a storm, with thunder so loud in my ears that I couldn't think straight and a deluge of icy water threatening to drown me at any moment. I couldn't outrun it.

I presented a good face to the world – at school, or away for weekends and holidays with my dad or grandparents. I would smile and pretend that nothing was wrong. I didn't want anyone to think I didn't enjoy being in their company. I adored my family and always valued time spent together. I forced myself to walk out the door, to say yes when all I wanted was to say no. At school I did my work, revised for my exams and was never rude to the teachers. And I developed quite a sarcastic wit to mask my feelings.

I remember walking to the shops with my mum one grey, drizzly day when I was about fifteen. We passed a group of girls I knew at the bus stop. 'We're catching the bus to York, want to come?' one of them asked. My mum nudged me forwards. I was uncertain but nodded, pleased to have been included. Mum put a twenty-pound note in my hand and waved as she headed home.

I felt awkward and tried to be flippant: 'I thought you'd forgotten who I was . . .'

'Thought you were too busy being a loner,' one girl said with a mock frown that broke into a smile.

'As if,' another said, pulling me into the shelter out of the rain.

*

It felt good to laugh and we had a fun day in York, wandering the historic walls and venturing down the Shambles' cobbled streets. As my friendships slowly reformed, further invitations came my way. I would go to watch a film at someone's house, or we would meet up and walk around the village – a circuit through the centre, down the road, past the primary school, along the lanes, through snickets and across fields until we arrived back where we'd started. The talk would be about trivial things – homework, books, boys and music, lots of music – but walking was a relief and being in the fresh air made everything seem so much more manageable.

I went for long walks by myself as well, usually after dinner in the cool evening air. I felt tiny and insignificant walking in the light of the moon, through fields undisturbed by the street lights of town, under trees casting shadows in the night, the sound of silence broken only by the hooting of an owl. I watched for shooting stars, hoping that they could fulfil my wishes. It was a chance to think and plan – and it would be with a heavy heart that I returned to my room, to sleep before I had to face a new day.

I found music helped too. I have always had music in my life, from Mum's LPs to my dad singing songs from musicals as we rode in the car together. I can remember my first cassette Walkman. It had two buttons and a volume control and my mum bought me a London Boys album that I played until I wore it out. From then on my headphones were always in, music blaring. As I got older, I used to listen to Guns N' Roses' 'November Rain' and Aerosmith's 'Amazing' on repeat, finding that the lyrics resonated with my feelings. I even wrote some of the lines down and then burned the pages. It might seem dramatic now but I found it therapeutic at the time. I hoped it would help to burn the emotions from my mind.

I understand now that I boxed my troubles up and

locked them away without really probing where the pain came from. I wanted to feel normal and appear as everyone else did. I've come to realise that if I were hiding something, maybe others were too. I have been trying to work it out for years but haven't got very far. I have slowly learned to know myself better though, both the good and the bad.

Looking back, I am surprised no one figured me out. I must have been very good at pulling the wool over people's eyes. But it wasn't a game. I sometimes sat in class watching people score their wrists with the point of their compass, in full view, just to prove they were cool enough or hard enough. I hated them because it seemed like a performance. I hurt myself to protect my sanity. I hid my scars so no one could see them – the cuts were small but the wounds were deep.

*

When the time came to choose what I wanted to do with my life, I struggled. I didn't really feel that I had found my talent or passion, and when I shared my ambitions with teachers, I was told that my grades weren't high enough, that I wasn't quite good enough. The wider world was a scary place and I had no idea where I fitted in. Everyone was being labelled again, this time by their career aspirations – doctor, vet, nurse, artist, musician – and they were starting to plan the next few years around these labels.

'I would like to be a writer,' I told our careers advisor.

'Journalism is a good career path,' she said. 'Why don't you look at doing a media course? You could get a placement at the local paper.'

'I don't want to write news, I want to write novels, books people want to read and keep, not tomorrow's chip paper,' I said.

'That is not a career, that is a dream,' she told me sternly before handing out some leaflets and sending me on my way.

I spent hours in the library researching different careers, trying to find a course or job that would grab my attention. But I drew a blank – nothing enticed me. Part of the problem was that I didn't feel especially good at anything. I was desperate for a talent or vocation, a way to make my mum proud, though I knew deep down she would be proud of me no matter what. But nothing ever stuck. I could play a little guitar and a little piano. I could sing and memorise lyrics, but my voice wasn't exceptional and my musical taste was so vast and varied, I didn't have the focus to dedicate to one style. What I liked to listen to changed – and still changes – with my mood, like the weather with the seasons. My mother taught me to cook and I could sew and draw and paint a bit, but I felt like a jack of all trades and a master of none. And yet, I couldn't shake the idea that there must be more to life, a role for me, a reason for my being.

I thought that my thing might be writing. For as long as I can remember, I have spent hours scribbling in notebooks and diaries. I wrote poems, stories and songs, copied quotations and kept a journal. I loved putting my thoughts down on paper and seeing where my imagination would take me. But I had been told that I wasn't good enough, that I had to be realistic. I tried really hard to fit in and do what was expected of me, but I always felt that I was in turmoil – that no one could really see me or help me to achieve all that I wanted to achieve.

Around this time, I headed out early one Sunday morning for a short walk in the morning air, the sun high in the sky, the milk van rattling down the road. The streets were quiet and there were only a few people about, buying the morning papers or walking their dogs. I stuck my headphones in and turned the volume to full blast. As I glanced up, I saw an elderly gentleman walking towards me, his eyes locking onto mine. I pulled one headphone out.

'You need more colour in your life,' he said with a slight smile.

I knew he didn't mean anything by it – he was a typical Yorkshireman with a friendly joke, though to some it might have seemed rude. I didn't like to think that I had let my mask slip, even for a moment, but as he waved goodbye and told me to have a nice day, I smiled. A genuine smile. Not simply a polite one. The village was full of characters, all memorable in their own way, all ready and waiting with an interested word if you took the time to glance in their direction and connect.

As I arrived home, my mum was making her morning cuppa. 'Do you want one, love?'

I nodded and took an old silver teaspoon from the drawer and held it out to her. 'What do you think I'll be when I am older?' I asked her.

She looked surprised at my question but was quick to answer. 'I know you will be anything you want to be.' She stirred the leaves. Tea was always made in the teapot, well-brewed. 'Water bewitched and tea be blessed,' she said. Every time we went to visit my mum's mum – my gran – we would dash inside out of the cold and she would make us a cup of tea and

I would hear those words muttered between them. They were comforting words.

'Do you know what? I think I will.' I felt suddenly weightless, as if a black cloud had lifted. Can a cup of tea really make everything better? Maybe it can.

*

So, the storm did not last for ever and I did manage to break free. Slowly, I began to feel that my life had meaning; that I was on a journey and had a future. There was no sudden epiphany, but my state of mind improved and light came into my world. I started to cope with my feelings a little better – they became subdued somehow with new thoughts and feelings pushing them aside – and the impulse to self-harm weakened and became less frequent. I found the strength to say I did not want that any more. I wanted to be strong. I wanted to get on rather than pretending.

Starting college helped enormously. I settled into a public services course and gained a good group of friends. The camaraderie between us created a sense of inclusion and trust. I chose the course because it covered such a broad range of subjects, so I could keep my options open. I studied psychology and criminology alongside first aid and outdoor adventures, including abseiling, orienteering and military training. The college was in York, which was two bus journeys away, but I didn't mind as it gave me the opportunity to listen to more music. I found it easier to be myself, perhaps because we were all in the same boat – everyone was new and no one had any preconceived ideas about each other. We came from different backgrounds and were all carving out different paths. I felt more comfortable about being shy and quiet when I realised no one was judging me. I would happily eat lunch with my new friends and join them on trips into town but I didn't feel bad about taking time out to be on my own.

I enjoyed disappearing to the quiet of the library especially – sometimes to do work or read, but I also signed up for a Yahoo account and would play games online and chat to people from all over the world. I made friends with a guy from Sheffield whose music taste matched mine in the sense he was completely obsessed with everything. He had real talent and was in a band and played guitar and drums and wrote his own pieces too. I could have talked to him for hours.

And I began to know myself better and learned to

accept my flaws. I am a pessimist – positive feelings get pushed down by the negative – and the glass with me is probably broken, not half empty. I expect the worst and wait for bad things to happen. I am competitive and a perfectionist, which is both a strength and a weakness. I am naturally insecure, forever needing validation and valuing the opinions of others more than I should. If I got nineteen out of twenty in a test, I would dwell on the one wrong answer, the mistake niggling away at me, driving me insane.

By noticing when my behaviour wasn't particularly healthy or helpful, I was able to call myself on it. Slowly, like climbing a ladder one rung at a time, my confidence improved – but I was careful not to take anything for granted until I got to the top and was able to stand on firm ground. It was only then that I felt able to throw away the shard hidden under my bed. I no longer needed it. I took the piece to a field a few miles away – the field with the 'walking tree' – and buried it there. The tree stands withered in the centre of an empty field surrounded by dykes. It grows crookedly across the ground, with twisted branches that reach out like gnarled claws, and a hollow trunk suggesting an old curved doorway, like a Hobbit hole. It has no leaves, even in the summer, and the whole field feels dead, as though nothing could live there: no greenery, no saplings, no leaves. As I buried the shard, it was as though I crouched in a charcoal drawing, my form blurred by thick black lines. I touched the bark – hard, cold and rough – and felt haunted, waiting for something to reach out and grab me. It was an eerie experience but rather fitting that this tree of nightmares should accept and hold my own nightmares. With every step away from the field, I felt lighter; it was incredibly liberating and over the next few weeks and months, as I worked hard at college and my friendships developed, I smiled from inside out.

When my eighteenth birthday came around, I actually felt like celebrating. It was a big occasion and I got dressed up, choosing to wear a skirt for the first time in a long time. We went out to my favourite restaurant, The Bayernstubl in Pocklington, for lunch. My dad came and my grandparents too. 'She's got legs,' my grandma gasped when she saw me. My grandad was proud to buy me my first legal drink. He joked that we were in a German restaurant drinking Australian lager and eating English food, as I sipped my drink and enjoyed a birthday meal of steak and chips. For the first time in my life, I had my dad on one side and my mum on the other. From the outside we would have looked like the perfect happy family. It was the best birthday present I could have asked for. My mum lit the candles on the cake and everyone sang 'Happy Birthday'. I went for a walk later, in the early evening sun, feeling content, rather than needing to get away, and looking forward to what tomorrow might bring.

*

I was eighteen, an adult at last, no longer lonely, and feeling much happier with life. I was also infatuated – with a guy from the RAF who had come to give a careers talk to our class one afternoon. Every girl had swooned over him, drooling on the tables as they asked question after question. The guys were full of admiration, all wanting to be him. I listened intently, not immune to his charms but not as forward as the others. As he finished his talk, his eyes locked onto mine. I quickly turned away but he stopped me on the way out.

'Fancy a drink?' he asked.

I stood, stunned briefly, before finding my voice. 'Is that allowed?' I glanced towards my tutor.

'I'm on leave, no law against it,' the soldier grinned.

My classes had finished for the day, so we headed into town and hit it off immediately, talking for hours. He was strong and charming – exactly what I needed – and he offered a life beyond the confines of the village and its surrounding area. His promise was only for a few weeks, after which he would have to return to his base and I would have to forget he had existed. But in those few weeks we spent every bit of free time together. He adored his car and would drive fast with the music blaring, usually Aerosmith's 'I Don't Want to Miss a Thing' on repeat. A romantic gesture, or perhaps he just really liked the song; I never asked. I couldn't help staring at him as he drove and he'd turn his head sometimes and catch me, chuckling to himself.

'You won't melt if you leave Yorkshire, you know,' he said one afternoon as we walked hand in hand through the city.

'I know,' I squeezed his hand. I knew he had seen much more of the world than I had but I wasn't embarrassed or ashamed. It had taken me a long time to feel comfortable in my skin and living in a Yorkshire community was a big part of that process. 'I am happy here.'

'In this location or with me?' he asked.

'Both,' I told him with a wry smile. 'But I'm aware we don't have long.' As he wrapped his arm around me and pulled me into his chest, I felt safe and the past magically disappeared, as though it had never happened.

I was young and giddy with first love. It was a whirlwind romance; everything I had ever dreamed about. He wrote me long letters, even though we would see each other most days, and I began to hope that we might be able to continue the relationship a bit longer. But when the dreaded day arrived and he packed his bags and drove off, it hit me really hard. I was crushed. I locked myself in my room, rereading his letters and gazing at our photos. He'd left one of his tops on my bed and I filled a box with snippets from our few weeks together.

My college friends were a little peeved I'd neglected them and I didn't have the energy or inclination to grovel for forgiveness, so I spent more time in the library, studying or chatting to my online friends. The next few weeks were difficult, but in the end life carried on as before. I still hoped that a letter would come, but I chose to focus on my studies rather than the loss I felt. He had promised me a few weeks, not for ever, and I knew deep down that it was a fleeting romance and I had to move on. And I did. I worked hard and achieved distinctions in my assignments. I was proud of my success.

*

One morning, I was heading to the library to submit my last piece of coursework when I opened my inbox to find an email from my Sheffield music friend with the subject heading: 'I NEED YOU'. He asked me to meet him off the Sheffield to York train at 10.37 the following morning. I sat staring at the email for a few minutes. We'd been talking for over a year and had exchanged pictures, so I felt like I knew him. He was important to me; if he needed me for some reason, then I would help. Ignoring the butterflies in my stomach – the doubts about how I felt about him and what he wanted from me, especially so soon after my soldier – I replied to reassure him that I would be there.

Next day I stood on the platform at York railway station and waited for his train to arrive. As the train pulled in, I saw him standing in the doorway. He was dressed all in black and looked ashen. I hugged him before he could even say hello. 'My mum died,' he told me, his voice breaking, 'in a car crash.' I don't know what I had expected, but not this. It was too awful to contemplate. I had no words for him, but as the silence stretched between us, he asked, 'Can we walk?' I released him and nodded. It was a long day. We walked a lot and listened to my Walkman. I could share my headphones but I didn't know what to say to make it better.

Over the next few weeks we spent more and more time together. I had never known grief, the unbearable sadness and anger, and although the loss wasn't mine to endure I struggled to make sense of it all. It was so cruel that she had been there one moment and gone the next. And now he had to move on. I tried to comfort him but everything I said sounded trite or clichéd. When I smiled or laughed, it seemed inappropriate, out of place. I wanted to be strong for him but found myself sinking into a depressive state of mind. I felt unable to cope and this led me back to self-harm. The familiarity of the process – the little cuts and sharp pain made with another shard of mirror – gave me back a feeling of control. And yet, the act disgusted me now and I felt so guilty, knowing that I had failed him and failed myself. As I sliced my flesh a little deeper each time, I sought a release that wouldn't come.

Then one time the blood kept flowing and with it the hate and pain and anger left my body. I got tired of holding on and drifted into semi-consciousness. I found myself at the walking tree in the black of night – chilled and trapped as the boughs wrapped around me, pulling me into the knotted bark, squeezing so tight I could feel my life ebbing away. Against the howling wind, the branches twisted and cut into my skin in all directions, and as my body slumped, limp, the village came alive in my mind. I could see friendly faces on a sunlit day – hellos and goodbyes from people going about their business; the lady setting up her fruit and veg, the newsagent taking in the morning papers; the man on the bicycle who always rang his bell, the jingle of the ice cream van – all the reasons I love this place I call home.

I woke gasping. I was terrified by the dried blood on my arms and the drips on the carpet that I knew would stain. My dream had been so vivid that although the sun was shining outside and the house was quiet, it felt very dark. I'd reached my lowest point, lying on the floor of my childhood bedroom, barely conscious, and I realised I couldn't take it any more. I did not want to feel this way and I did not want to die. So I grabbed a bag, stuffed the broken compact in my pocket and did the only thing that seemed possible: I walked out the door and away from my life. I threw the compact in a rubbish bin and then walked and walked and kept on walking until I found myself on a road that I did not know.

I sent an email to my friend from Sheffield – a copy of the one he sent me, asking him to meet me off the train, to be there for me as I was for him. I phoned my mum when I arrived and explained my intention to stay for a few days. But a few days became a few weeks as our friendship grew into something more romantic. I was struggling to decipher between love and sympathy, and felt angry that our relationship – which held huge promise – had been forced by circumstance to become serious so soon. But we came to rely on each other; he helped me to find a flat in the city and I supported him, listening as he tried to work through his loss.

Sheffield was overwhelming at first, as I wasn't used to such busy streets and the rush of traffic, but it was a beautiful city too, and away from its imposing buildings and impressive steel structures, it had quieter leafy suburbs and a real sense of history. I rented a room in a shared house in one of the suburbs and managed to find a job – rather astonishingly for a village girl – as a croupier in a casino. I never dreamt I would be capable of such a role. I saw the job advertised not fully knowing what it was; otherwise I might not have applied at all! I quickly became known as 'mouse' because I was so quiet. But it was exciting and fast-paced and I enjoyed being part of the team. And my boss took me under her wing, teaching me roulette and poker: the rules, the odds and the payouts, so I was able to call 'bets please' loud and proud every night.

My housemates – three guys and a girl – were easy to get along with and we would stay up chatting on my nights off (the downside to the casino was that it altered my body clock for ever). But as I spread my wings, I began to feel suffocated by my relationship. There was an unhealthy dependence on both sides and the constant phone calls and texts, the need to know where I was, where he was, it all became too much. I didn't feel in control.

One evening I knocked a glass over as I tried to reach for it on the top shelf of the kitchen cupboard. It fell to the floor, shattering on the tiled surface, and there reflecting in the broken shards was the potential to find relief. I wanted to feel that sense of calm. I held a slither of glass in my hand, staring at it glinting in the light, weighing up my options. Here was an opportunity to take control. But instead I dropped the shard and dashed out into the cool night air, walking quickly as the tears rolled down my cheeks. I wanted to be free of the depression, of the temptation to do myself harm. I hadn't expected it to reappear without warning. I knew I had to make some changes. I had given the relationship my best shot, but in the end it wasn't enough.

'Thank you for being there for me,' he said as we parted and hugged each other goodbye. He handed me a cassette tape of his music, including a song he had written for me, and with tears in my eyes I walked away.

*

Over the following weeks, everything settled down. There was a sense of freedom in the city. Holme had seemed claustrophobic at times, the walls closing in with no feeling of escape, but in Sheffield I had time and space to process my emotions. No one judged me for having a bad day or even a bad week. The hardest thing I found was admitting that the impulse to self-harm would always be there, lingering in the background, an inner demon that wasn't going to go away, but when I accepted that, I realised I was in control.

And then one evening my acceptance was tested as my housemates and I were chatting and the subject of self-harm came up. One of my housemates told us that the girl he'd been seeing had these slash marks across her arms, scars that she had tried to hide but that he had seen. I knew instantly what he meant. I tried to remain impassive but snapped angrily when another housemate said it was just attention seeking. I think they were all a little surprised that I was upset.

One by one, they drifted off to bed. It was two in the morning, but I was still wide awake.

'Why do you do it?' murmured the only guy left in the room. I looked at him, puzzled for a moment. 'Why do you self-harm?' he clarified.

'I don't,' I said, which was the truth by this point.

'OK. So why did you do it?'

I found that I didn't have the words to deny it.

'It's all right. I guessed – you reacted so strongly just now.' He shrugged, aware of my discomfort, trying not to make a big deal about it.

'It's a release,' I said simply, not wanting to reveal

too much but also feeling a certain relief in speaking about it at last.

A few days later, he told me he had tried it for himself. I was speechless. I couldn't understand why anyone would choose to try it and told him this. He said he'd wanted to understand, but couldn't bring himself to make the cut in the end and that he respected me for being so brave. I was livid and told him it wasn't a rational decision; it came from a place of desperation and pain. We talked for a while and I found that I no longer cared about saying too much. He was a good friend and didn't judge me, and by telling him about it I realised that I had survived.

*

Years went by before I found the strength to return to the village for any extended period of time. Holme was my safety net – familiar and comfortable – but it held bad memories, along with the good, and I was afraid that I would regress if I went back. The more I thought about it, the more the village tended to reflect and amplify my own feelings. During my early childhood it was filled with sunshine and fun, but when I started to feel sad it became very cold, a lonely place to be. When I wanted people to notice me, it seemed that no one did; and when I wanted to hide away, I felt like all eyes were on me, the centre of the village's attention.

I wanted to return a changed person – to make my family proud and show everyone how successful and grown-up I'd become – but I knew deep down that I was just the same girl who went away. A little happier and freer, but I feared that returning to my mum's house and my childhood bedroom with all of my books and my posters would somehow trap me, dragging me back to a time I'd rather forget. But I also knew that I couldn't run for ever and at some point I'd have to stand still and face up to my demons.

I drifted back and forth for a few years, making my peace with the village, but never quite settling there, or anywhere, never committing to calling a place my home. I felt that I didn't need a home. I was enjoying the freedom of not being tied to a place, to a person, to a set idea of myself. I had a few relationships, but nothing serious or lasting. I remember one chap saying I was witty and beautiful – a snippet I have locked away in my mind for moments of self-doubt, days when I look in the mirror and wish to be anyone but me. Those days haven't disappeared completely. No matter how happy I am – and I am now happy – I know that I will always have to be vigilant, to be careful.

HOLME TODAY IS not the place I once knew it to be. Many of my childhood haunts have gone and where green fields once were there are now houses. Footpaths have disappeared, snickets and ginnels blocked off so gardens could be extended, driveways created and new roads laid down. It is a commuters' paradise: a rural village location with the convenience of a town and easy access to the main roads leading to Leeds, Hull and York.

Shops have closed, many have changed hands, the Station Inn, where I spent some great nights listening to music and playing pool with friends is long gone, while the dairy factory – Dale Farm in my day – has a new name but still gives out its sweet cocoa smell. The post office is still there, but now there's a cash machine too. Ye Olde Red Lion will always be the place for a good Sunday roast, although I don't know whether they still make my favourite lattice-topped apple pie with cinnamon and sultanas which always came with a jug of cream. The Blacksmith Arms, the Hare and Hounds remain, as does the village hall, where I used to go to Brownies and Guides, and the social club with bingo on Friday and country and western dances on Saturday nights. I remember darts and snooker competitions too. The village store, the butcher's and bakery are all still there, and in the centre of the village, there is the green with the tree that is always adorned with lights at Christmas, and the telephone box, which is rarely used now. Despite the change, the heart stays the same.

I still visit regularly, to see my mum, my brother and my nieces and nephews, friends still live in nearby towns, including my childhood best friend – my 'twin' – we are just as much trouble now as we were then, so perhaps the nickname holds. I often take my children and they enjoy many of the things that I used to: running in the fields and along the railway tracks, over stiles and through kissing gates, climbing trees and sitting in the grass making daisy chains. They cheer as I did as they run past the grounds of Holme Rovers, and they love playing at the park, although with a zip wire, climbing frame and obstacle course of tyres and chains, not to mention the wooden tractor and trailer ride, it's advanced a little since I was a girl. At Easter, we take decorated eggs to the top of Church Hill and roll them down, and each winter, I hope for snow so I can take them sledging. We try to attend the annual summer gala and I introduce my children to people who say, 'I knew your mummy when she was a little girl'. The ice cream van, tombola, face painting, bouncy castle and hook a duck: my children love it all. Even though we now live in a time of technology, simple things still please.

Although it would have been a great place to raise my family, I have put down roots elsewhere, in another village, not too far away, one that I hadn't even heard of before my husband and I went to view a house there. It was a comfort to return to village life. I never felt at home in the city, not really, and although my husband is Sheffield-born, he has also come to love village life.

We met in a pub not far from my shared house in 2004. I would never have thought that calling in for a quiet drink would change my life. I was sitting perched at the end of the bar while he poured me a drink. I reached for the glass before he could pass it over. 'That for me?' I asked. 'Hey, be nice to me. I'm hungover,' he whispered. And that was all the excuse I needed for a bit of banter with him – he should have guessed I was trouble! Within a month we were seeing each other every night and I found myself glued to my phone waiting for his texts and calls. I knew that I had met a wonderful man, a wonderful Yorkshire lad who would be loyal and steadfast and true. He made, and still makes, me feel beautiful inside and out. It was frightening at first, to love someone so instinctively that I became helpless, and I was terrified of losing control and my independence. But I felt safe enough with him to share the secrets from my past, and it has only strengthened our relationship. He knows me better than anyone and though he will joke, 'You're a closed book in a locked box', I do open up to him. I never wanted to need someone, to rely on someone, but having him by my side makes the world a brighter place.

Our new village is a lot smaller than Holme and it has a lovely sense of inclusion and community, a friendly welcome and warmth about it. Old stone cottages stand amongst modern semis, with larger farmhouses and barn conversions further out. We have fields at the end of the garden and quite often a cow will stick her head over the back fence to steal apples from the tree or bread from the bird table. My children love running down the garden to feed her leaves and grass cuttings. There is an old steam railway at the bottom of the road, which reminds me of the old Holme Moor railway. We take family walks along the canal and through woods, kicking up leaves or crunching them underfoot, climbing on old slag heaps from forgotten mines and scrambling over drystone walls. We enjoy picnics in the summer sunshine and pick blackberries in September. Our children attend the local primary school, the very same school their grandad, my father-in-law, attended when he was a lad, and although the old school building has been knocked down and a new one built, I like the family connection.

I may have left Holme, but I haven't left Yorkshire and don't think I ever will. It is a beautiful county, especially in spring when the green fields glisten with drops of dew in the morning sun and daisies and daffodils are scattered across the meadows. There is a thicket of bluebells nearby, and a wood where branches tangle and bud with explosions of pink blossom, the locations of which will remain my secret. I like listening to the sparrows chirping and watching the bees buzz from flower to flower in the summer, seeking the pollen that lingers in the air like fairy dust. I love it here and could ride my bicycle for miles – down lanes and up hills – enjoying the freedom and beauty of these parts. I belong to the landscape and the horizon and am happy when I have space to dream.

Holme will forever have a special place in my heart. I love visiting and driving through on trips to the seaside – as we approach the Howden turn-off on the M62 and see the blue metal of Boothferry Bridge over the river, I feel a comforting familiarity. But I know that I am just passing through. I am not stopping. The village feels distant from me now: a different place, a different time and a different me. I wonder whether the connection will fade further when the ties I have there no longer remain. I will have to hold the memories dear.

And yet, I know that I must be careful with memories. Like books and music, they offer an alternative to reality, a chance to lose myself in another life. I listen to music to bring tears to my eyes or to spark anger or a burst of happiness, to feel confident and ready to face the world, or to wallow sometimes. There is nothing wrong with wallowing, as long as I can eventually break free from it – have a good cry and then move on. I try hard not to lock my feelings away now, lest they bubble under the surface, allowing the darkness in. I know it will never be gone completely but I no longer seek it out. And I do not look back with regret either. I cannot change the past. Living through the spells of depression and grief have made me who I am today; I am stronger because of the battles I have faced. It was a dark tunnel to go through, but there was light at the end of it.

I have come to realise that you have to allow yourself to be happy, to enjoy the present moment, to surround yourself with loved ones, to make peace with the past and not worry so much about the future.

I was perusing the bookshelves of a local charity shop recently, looking for a new novel to read, when an old Hans Christian Andersen book with a brown-leather binding caught my eye. As I blew dust off the cover and pulled it from the shelf, a piece of paper fell out with the words: 'Life is not about waiting for the storm to pass . . . It is about learning to dance in the rain' – a motivational quote by Vivian Greene – written beneath a sketch of a girl holding an umbrella under a cloud. I stood holding this rather crumpled bit of paper and realised I had spent a long time wishing my life away, thinking it will be better tomorrow and I will be happier next week. It is OK sometimes not to be OK. Rather than waiting for life to change, I had to get on and live it. I put the paper in my pocket, paid for the book and wandered home.

A bit of water would never stop us Yorkshire folk: come rain or shine we embrace life, so with that in mind, I grabbed my umbrella and rather than waiting for the storm to pass, I learned to dance in the rain.

HOMETOWN TALES

AVAILABLE NOW FROM W&N